Selfiers: Sealed with Images

Xu Lei ⋈ He Bo

自拍者:
尺笺传影

La Maison de Z

何 博
许 雷

Editor's Note III

1
The First Letter from Xu Lei 1

2
The Fisrt Letter from He Bo 11

3
The Second Letter from Xu Lei 27

4
The Second Letter from He Bo 39

5
The Third Letter from Xu Lei 59

6
The Third Letterfrom He Bo 77

7
The Fourth Letter from Xu Lei 97

8
The Fourth Letter from He Bo 115

9
The Fifth Letter from Xu Lei 133

10
The Fifth Letter from He Bo 151

About the Author 169

目录

编者按..................III

一
来自许雷的第一封信..................1

二
来自何博的第一封信..................11

三
来自许雷的第二封信..................27

四
来自何博的第二封信..................39

五
来自许雷的第三封信..................59

六
来自何博的第三封信..................77

七
来自许雷的第四封信..................97

八
来自何博的第四封信..................115

九
来自许雷的第五封信..................133

十
来自何博的第五封信..................151

作者小传..................169

Editor's Note

We really appreciate the love and support of our faithful readers, who have contributed to the success of La Maison de Z for five years since its beginning. The growth of our magazine is accompanied by a consistent flow of readers' submissions and letters, from which we select the outstanding photographic works and articles to publish in the "Another Glance" and "Outside of the Wall" sections of each issue in order to build a bridge among our readers.

In this special issue, we present an innovative project from the submissions, which includes a significant amount of self-portraits and handwritten letters from two amateur photographers, He Bo and Xu Lei, who are based in two separate regions of China but connect through their exchange.

He Bo, originally from Sichuan Province, is now serving in the army at the border of China; while Xu Lei, from Shandong Province, is currently teaching at a university in Fujian. These two amateur photographers correspond via letters and photos to share their thoughts and experiences around the concept of the "self-portrait," which is a relatively novel form of photography at the moment. As they examine the definition of self-portrait and its relevant context and techniques, they also show us the local customs of both the Nanshan and Fuzhou in their photos and letters.

Their self-initiated inquiry is a reflection of people's growing participation in a wide range of cultural and artistic activities after the reform and opening up policy. We believe that photography, as a free form of art, will one day grow in popularity and we look forward to discovering more and more experimental projects that step outside the box.

Editor-in-Chief of La Maison de Z
November 1983

编者按

本刊创刊五年,顺利发展至今,离不开读者诸君的喜爱与支持,编辑部荣幸、感激之至。读者源源不断的投稿和来信伴随着本刊的成长,基于此,本刊得以选取优秀的摄影作品和文章,在每期的"读者佳作""读者园地"等栏目里刊登,为读者之间的交流搭建平台。

本期增刊,编辑部将完整呈现一组颇具新意的读者投稿——包含许多张摄影自拍像和大量手写信件,它们出自两位身处祖国两地、过往未曾谋面的摄影爱好者何博和许雷之手。

何博来自四川,是一名驻扎祖国边疆的文艺兵;许雷生长于山东,作为老师在福建一所大学教书育人。两位业余摄影师相互写信、寄送照片,围绕"自拍"这一当下还很新的创作方式交流经验和想法。在探讨自拍和相关摄影文化知识的同时,这些照片和信件也向我们展示了新疆南山地区和福州两地的风土人情。

这两位自发的实践,是改革开放后,人民群众开始参与到丰富多彩的文化艺术活动中开拓眼界、陶冶情操的一块切面。我们相信,摄影作为一种民主的艺术形式,普及程度一定会越来越高。我们期待从读者那里看到更多、更有意思的摄影实践成果!

本刊编辑部
1983 年 11 月

VI

Selfiers: Sealed with Images

何博兄：

展信好！许久未见，近况如何？

暑期即将结束，前几日李明、王伟来榕相聚，我带他们到西湖一游，拍摄了些风景留影等，期间在玉带桥边三人自拍合影一张，附赠于您留念。已过处暑，但福州暑意未消，且拍此照时已临近当午，光线强烈，脸部阴影稍显浓重，背景景物对比也较浅，颇有"浓墨重彩"的意境，但是这貌似并不是拍摄们家留影的好时机，权当经验教训了。

提到西湖，大多想到的是杭州的西湖，却不知福州也有一西湖，且已有1700多年的历史了，是福州现今保留最完整的一座古典园林。福州西湖为晋太康三年（公元282年）郡守严高所凿，清道光八年（公元1828年）林则徐为湖岸砌砌石，重新修建，至1914年辟为公园。如您有机会来榕，可同游西湖。

从古人水边顾影自怜，到现今地对镜梳妆。我想，我们利用相机留下自己的影像也出于类似心理，

当亲游说，不在杭州西湖也未去过。

来自许雷的第一封信

何博兄：

展信好！许久未见，近况如何？

暑期即将结束，前几日李明、王伟来榕相聚，我带他们到西湖一游，拍摄了些风景、留影等，期间在五门桥边三人自拍合影一张，附赠于你留念。虽已过处暑，但福州暑意未消，且拍此照时已经临近当午，光线强烈，脸部阴影稍显浓重，背景之物对比也较强，颇有"浓墨重彩"的意境，但是这貌似并不是拍摄人像留影的好时机，权当经验教训了。

提到西湖，大多想到的是杭州的西湖，却不知福州也有一西湖[1]，且已有1700多年的历史了，是福州现今保留最完整的一座古典园林。福州西湖为晋太康三年（公元282年）郡守严高所凿，清道光八年（公元1828年）林则徐为湖岸砌石，重新修建，至1914年辟为西湖公园。如你有机会来榕，可同游西湖。

从古人水边顾影自怜，到现今的对镜梳妆。我想，我们利用相机留下自己的影像也出于类似心理，以期用照片这种载体留下自己青春美丽的瞬间吧，多年后翻看相册，还能感受到当时拍照时的心境和状态，定有一番趣味吧。

粉碎"四人帮"后，国家发展逐步步入正轨，改革开放也让我们看到了未来的曙光，经济水平的提升、物质条件的富足，能让更多的普通老百姓享受到摄影这种方式带给我们的便利，不用再颇有仪式感地踏入照相馆，才能得到一张端庄的个人留影或合影。像现在的我们，都拥有了自己的相机，外出游览、亲朋欢聚、单位活动等，均可让相机随行，留下诸多美好瞬间，而且画面内容更趋活泼，不再呆板端庄，多了几分生活气息。

随着摄影知识的普及，先进照相器材的引进和研制，具有一定知识水平的人经过学习后即可掌握一般的拍摄技术，为个人生活带来乐趣的同时还能留下珍贵的家庭影像。不过，我觉得现今的摄影工具还稍显繁琐，比如一个人自拍留影时，需先取景、对焦、调整光圈快门等，等开启自拍定时，自己跑到先前预想位置中，难免会产生些许偏差，不能十全十美。但是，快门开启的瞬间，拍摄下的又正好是那时那刻最真实的状态，或刚到位置站（坐）定，神情期待，或匆忙狼狈，但是不管如何，均要等到冲洗之后才会最终显现，其间过程还融合了长久的期待与盼望，我想，自拍的乐趣此为其一吧。我们能否预想：在不久的将来，随着技术的进步，能否会出现一种更加便捷的摄影器材[2]，能够看到自拍的效果甚至随时自己控制快门来拍摄？让我们共同期待吧！

此致，顺颂近安！

许 雷
1982年8月27日于福州

---

1 ［何博注］当去游玩，不过杭州西湖也未去过。

2 何博注：何时我辈可拥有一台POLAROID？（北京的首长那台确实太有趣了）

以期用照片这种载体留下自己青春美丽的瞬间吧，多年后翻开看相册，还能感受到当时拍照时的心境和状态，定有一番趣味吧。

　　粉碎"四人帮"后，国家发展逐步走入正轨，改革开放也让我们看到了未来的曙光。经济水平的提升，物质条件的富足，能让更多的普通老百姓享受到摄影这种方式带给我们的便利，不用再频奔仪式感的踏入照相馆，才能得到一些端庄的个人留影或合影。像现在的我们，都拥有了自己的相机，外出游览、亲朋欢聚、单位活动等均可让相机伴随行，留下诸多美好瞬间，而且画面内容更趋活泼，不再单板端庄，多了几分生活气息。

　　随着摄影知识的普及，先进照相器材的引进和研制，具有一定知识水平的人经过学习后即可掌握一般的拍摄技术，为个人生活带来乐趣的同时也能留下珍贵的家庭影像。不过，我觉得现今的摄影工具还稍显繁琐，比如一个人自拍的影时，需先取景对焦，调整光圈快门等，再开启自拍的定时，自己跑到事前预想的景里中，难免会产生些许偏差，不能十全十美，但是，快门开启的瞬间，拍摄下的又正好是那时那刻最真实的状态。或刚到位置站（坐）定，神情期待，或匆忙狼狈，但是不管如何，均要等到冲洗之后才会最终呈现，其间过程还饱含了长久的期待的盼望。我想，自拍的乐趣也为其一吧。我们能否预想：在不久的将来，随着技术的进步，能否会出现一种更加便捷的摄影器材，能够看到自拍的效果更能随时自己控制快门来拍摄？让我们共同期待吧！

此致，顺颂近安！

何时我辈可拥有一台
POLAROID？

许雷

（北京的首长那些确实太有趣了）1982年8月27日于福州

830063

寄：新疆维吾尔自治区乌鲁木齐市乌鲁木齐县南山小渠子村 W6619 号部队
电影组

何 博 （同志）收

350025
福建省福州市仓山区二桥亭33号 林 城

Dear He Bo,

I hope this letter finds you well. I haven't heard from you in a while. How is everything?

Summer vacation is coming to an end. Li Ming and Wang Wei came to Fuzhou a few days ago. I brought them to the West Lake. Attached to the letter is a souvenir for you, which is one of the group portraits we took near the Wumen Bridge.

Although the End of Heat had passed, the summer heat was still here. The portrait was taken shortly before noon when the sunlight was still harsh. As a result, the shadow on our faces is quite heavy and so is the contrast in the background, giving the picture an unexpected touch. It was probably not the right time to shoot portraits and that was the lesson learned.

When it comes to West Lake, most people think of the one in Hangzhou, but many are unaware that there is also a West Lake Park in Fuzhou which dates back more than 1700 years. It was built by Yan Gao, the local governor of the Jin Dynasty (282 AD), refurbished by Lin Zexu under the Qing Dynasty (1828 AD), opened to the public in 1914 as West Lake Park, and is by far the best-preserved classical garden in Fuzhou. If you ever come visit, we should go check it out.

When looking into the past, I notice that our ancestors used to look at themselves by the water while we now dress in front of the mirror. I suppose we take portraits of ourselves with cameras for a similar reason and that is to capture and retain our special moments. It's certainly rewarding to journey back in time when we look at them years afterward.

Following the downfall of the Gang of Four, the country's development gradually got on the right track. The reform and opening-up policy has also provided us with a glimpse of the future. The improvement in economic and material conditions has made photography more and more accessible to ordinary people. The ceremonious act of going to the studio to have a portrait or a group photo is no longer the only option. For example, now that we already have our own cameras, we may use them to capture the lovely moments when we go sightseeing, hang out with friends or families, or attend work events. The photo scenes are becoming more dynamic and lively, while also getting less serious.

Thanks to advances in photographic literacy and the development of camera equipment, anyone with a basic understanding of photography can easily master some general shooting techniques by taking on an apprenticeship. It seasons our daily life while also preserving precious family memories.

However, I believe the cameras today are still a bit bulky. For example, in order to take a self-portrait, we must first take care of framing, focus, and exposure before setting up the timer. While we sprint to the intended spot, imperfections are also finding their way into the final result. Yet, what is captured at the moment through the shutter is the most realistic state possible at the time: It doesn't matter if you're ready to pose or not, looking intrigued or hasty.

Besides, there is no way to escape the long wait for film development. The whole process embraces anticipation and patience, which, I believe, is also one of the factors that contribute to the fun of taking self-portraits.

Can we envision more convenient camera equipment in the near future, along with technological advancements, that allow us to see the final result of taking a self-portrait or even control the shutter from a distance at any time? This is really something to look forward to.

I hope to hear from you soon.

All the best,

Xu Lei
August 27, 1982, Fuzhou

二

许雷兄

见信甚慰，犹见得李明、王伟二人依旧容光焕发，不犹由得忆起那年我等相聚之光景。感谢赠照片于我，你所说的泼墨重彩你说在此念想中再为合适不过，颇能感受到南方夏日之酷。

讲起福州西湖，以前不甚了解，许雷兄若有得闲暇，盼多有好照片以饱眼福。

关于粉碎"四人帮"至今已六年，我等新近

来自何博的第一封信

许雷兄：

见信甚慰，尤见得李明、王伟二人依旧容光焕发，不由得忆起那年我等相聚之光景。感谢赠照片予我，你所说的"浓墨重彩"体现在此合影中再为合适不过，颇能感受到南方夏日之酷。

讲起福州西湖，以前不甚了解，许雷兄若有得闲晰，盼多有好照片[3]以饱眼福。

关于粉碎"四人帮"，至今已六年，要是四人帮继续执政[4]，我等新近摄影者也无如今这宽松的创作环境。大幸。你可从我寄予你的那张我与战友焦钢之合影看出如今我们连队中拍照时的氛围。照片拍于稍早，春天，部队组织文艺兵去往北京参观学习。一日登八达岭长城，途中觅得一无人处，便支起部队的海鸥4A相机。由于出公差需要记录正事，所以此次携带的胶卷负片不少，时不时可以匀一些出来供留念照之用。

设置耗时，战友亦各自休整，故自拍实乃上策，顺便检验一番前些日子间断练着的自拍技巧。那日我心情极好，奈何身旁焦兄情绪不高，对我提出在照片里做些怪样之建议也不怎么感兴趣。所以最后的照片就成了你所看到的这样。你寄给我的自拍合影亦然，当几个人同时要出现在镜头里时，怎么样跟其他人沟通，以使他们愿意依照摄影师的想法来配合，这个是我一直在想的。焦钢兄平时与我关系甚好，但每有合影便严肃起来，此次摆拍也如此。

另一张随信附上的照片是夏初时，我找另一位战友刘德彪一起合作完成的。他与我一样，是都在电影组里担任放映员，其人活泼，易相处。与他的这张自拍合影实际上是部队的任务之一，给各个文艺组拍摄宣传照，所以你可以看出现场是有人工布光的。当然这张照片不能交给领导，因为我看了镜头了。还会有其他组的照片，有的是我另外参加的，将来再寄给你看。

你谈到的关于将来较为便捷的摄影器材可以方便自拍，尤其是能够立刻看到效果，这一点我也非常期待。前些日子在北京时，有幸随长官拜访其年轻时的首长，在首长家中见得一新式相机。时间上倒不新，七十年代所产，但于我而言实为首见。此相机为美国所产，名为POLAROID，便是拍摄之后片刻可出相片的器械。

奈何不知购得渠道，且囊中羞涩，暂无法尝试之。不过，我亦相信经年之后，此种相机将逐渐成为我等爱摄影者的必备物件，亦能走进广大百姓的家中。试想人人皆有自拍利器，在聚会旅游当下便有照片可供留念收纳，岂不美哉？

文行至此，营灯将熄。祝诸事顺利，安好。盼复。

何 博
1982年9月5日于乌鲁木齐

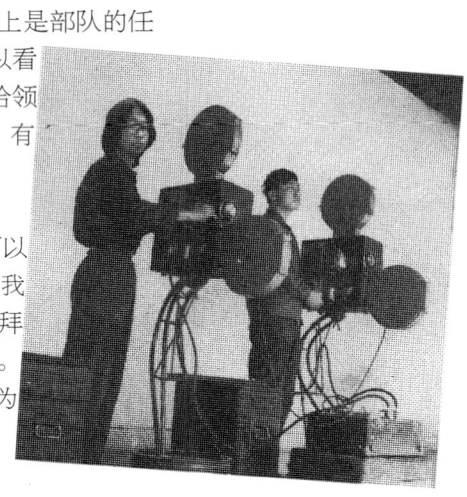

---

3 ［编者注］许雷着重圈出这五个字
4 ［编者注］此句为何博书写时遗漏

摄影者也无此宽松的创作环境。大幸，你可以我寄予你的那张我与战友焦钢之合影看出如今我们连队中拍照时的氛围。照片拍于暮春天。部队组织去芦沟桥北京参观学习一日，登八达岭长城，途中觉得一无人处，便支起部队的海鸥4A相机。由于出公差需要记录严事，所以此次携带的胶卷贡片不少，时不时可以匀一些出来供留念照之用。设置秒时，战友亦各自待整，故自拍实不上乘，顺便检验一番前些日子间断练着的自拍技巧。那日我心情极好，亲侄身旁焦兄情绪不高，对我提出在照片里做些怪样之建议也不怎么感兴趣。所以最后的照片就成了你所看到的这样。你寄给我的自拍合影亦然，当几父同时要出现在镜头里时，怎么样跟其他人沟通，以使他们愿意依照摄影师的想法来配合，这个是我一直在想的。黛钢兄平时与我关系基好，但年有合影便平素起来，此次摆拍也如此。另一张随信附上的照片是夏初时我另在成发刘德超一起合作完成的。他与我一样，都在便好组里担任放映员，其人活泼，易相处，与他敏注册自拍合影。实际上是部队的任务之一，给各个文艺组招摄宣传照，所以你可以看出现场是有人工布光的。当然这张照片不允许交给领导，因为我看了镜头了。还会有其他组的照片，有的是我另外参加的，将来再寄给你看。

你谈到的关于将来较为便捷的摄影器材可以方便自拍，尤其是能够立刻看到效果，这一点我也非常期待。前些二日在北京时，有幸随长官年访其年轻时的首长，在首长家中见得一新型相机。时间上倒不新，七十年代所产，但于我而言实为首见。此相机为美国所产，名为POLAROID，便是拍摄之后片刻可出相片的器械。奈何不知购得渠道,且囊中羞涩,暂无法尝试之。不过,我亦相信经年之后,此种相机将逐渐成为我等爱摄影者的必备物件,亦能走进广大百姓的家中。试想人人皆有自拍利器,在聚会旅游当下便有照片可供绍余收纳,岂不美哉?

文行至此,营灯将熄。祝诸事顺利,安好。盼复。

何博

1982年9月5日于乌鲁木齐

福建省福州市仓山区上三路壹拾贰号 福建师范大学

许霆（同志）收
350007

新疆维吾尔自治区乌鲁木齐市
乌鲁木齐县南山小派子村W66号牧民电影组
何博贵

21 Xu Lei He Bo

Dear Xu Lei,

Thanks for your letter. I'm glad to see that Li Ming and Wang Wei are doing well. I can't help but feel nostalgic when I think back on our time together. And thank you for the photo. There are no better words to describe it than "an unexpected touch." I can totally imagine the sweltering heat of a southern summer.

Speaking of Fuzhou West Lake, I didn't know much about it before. If you have time to take more photos of it, it would be a wonderful delight for me to see them.

Regarding the Gang of Four, it has been six years since its downfall, without which we wouldn't have been able to benefit from such a relaxed and free creative environment at the time as emerging photographers. We're lucky.

You may get an idea of the presence of photography in the company from the photo I'm sending you of myself and my comrade Jiao Gang. It was taken in early spring. Our company had organized a study trip to Beijing. One day on our journey up the Badaling Great Wall, I stumbled upon an empty spot and set up the company's Seagull 4A camera. Since I was responsible for recording work-related events during the trip, I packed a lot of films with me, and as a result, I was able to take some souvenir photos from time to time.

It always took me a while to set up the camera, and in the meantime, other comrades were enjoying their breaks. I found it a convenient time to take some self-portraits and to put my skills to the test, which I had been doing on the side for a while.

That day, I was in quite a good mood, but Jiao Gang, on the other hand, was not. He was uninterested in my idea to take a funny photo, so as you can see, this is the final result. Likewise, the group portrait you sent me is in the same boat, which makes me wonder how to communicate with other participants so that they can collaborate better with the photographer when making a group portrait.

Jiao Gang is usually very close to me, but whenever we pose for a photo together, he gets uncomfortable, which happened again this time.

The other photo attached to this letter was taken in early summer with the help of another comrade, Liu Debiao. We are both projectionists in the film crew. He is very outgoing and easy to get along with. This self-portrait with him was actually one of the company's assignments, which was to take publicity photos of different creative teams. So you can see we had studio lighting for the photo. But since I was looking at the camera

by accident as opposed to looking sideways like Liu Debiao, I won't submit it to the leaders. There will be photos of other teams as well, some of which I was also a member of. I'll send them to you in the future.

I'm particularly intrigued by your thoughts on the future of more convenient camera equipment that will make it easier to take self-portraits, especially if the results can be seen right away.

When I was in Beijing the other day, I had the pleasure of meeting my leader's previous commander. In the home of the commander, I noticed a new camera made in the late 1970s, which wasn't actually new at the time. It was, however, a first for me. The camera was called Polaroid and was manufactured in the United States. It was the type of instant camera that could create a chemically developed print shortly after taking the photo.

Sadly, I didn't know where to get it and I wasn't sure whether I could afford it, so there was no way to try it for the time being.

However, I believe that as time passes, this type of camera will become a must-have for us amateur photographers. It will eventually make its way into the homes of the general public. Wouldn't it be wonderful if everyone had a handy tool to capture moments of gatherings and trips right away?

I have to end here since the lights will be out soon. I can't wait to hear from you.

Best of luck,

He Bo
September 5, 1982, Urumqi

3
三

The Second Letter from Xu Lei

第 1 页

何博兄：

来信已于前几日收悉，特别是看到信中所附的两张照片，甚感亲切。

古人常说"见字如面"，但是我感觉这个说法在照片面前还是稍显逊色了。文字虽为信息传递的重要手段，但是文字要经过写作者的思考—表达，读者的阅读—理解等环节，难免出现偏差，但是照片对于观众来说就是看到的实实在在存在的东西，具体且形象，从拍摄者到观看者的传递过程中，信息到达率高，我想这也是摄影术之所以能诞生的原始动力吧。

近几日一直记得你信中提及的想让我多寄几张西湖照片与你，于是几天前一个下午独自一人到西湖一游，拍些西湖近照，赠一张在更衣亭附近的自拍倒影与你，更衣亭始建于五代，相传闽王王延钧每与王后金凤及宫娥乘船游湖时，在此更衣休息，因此得名。此处客照相馆摆拍者为游人拍照者甚多，左为西湖比较有代表性的景致了。在照片背景中你区可以看到上次寄给你的照片中拍照的地点玉汀桥。此次自拍较为顺利，

公文纸 →

第 2 页

园在湖边有一长条石凳，以此为参照物，相机参数设置上就更有些把握了，因为相机支起固定后，石凳在取景框中的位置是固定的，离相机的距离也是一定的，所以构图、对焦不会出现太大偏差。因取景构图需要，相机机位较低，有一定角度的仰拍，所以拍出来我还略显高大了些呢。

我包里也还有两张今年春季登鼓山时候的自拍留影，一并寄于你留念。第一张是在鼓山涌泉寺，从迴龙阁为背景，背靠放生池栏杆拍摄的。涌泉寺为福建名刹，历史悠久，始建于783年，时至今日，香火一直甚旺，广为僧侣或是代表性的景点，当年马噶尔尼.汤姆逊游历福州时也在此地拍了不少照片。照片中另外一人为我的好友苏德旺，他最近喜得一子，故同行到此烧香。时至中午，我们饮毕开之时，苏兄提议合影一张，故我架起相机，指挥苏兄站定，然后取景、调焦、定时，按照预想，我站在苏兄左边，故得此合影。我觉得你来信中也提及自拍时和合影者的互动问题，我觉得其实合影者可以作为取景构图时的一个很好的参照物，按照自己的意图指挥其站位或姿势，设想我们本人也在合影者的边上或某个位置真正定位后，拍摄

第 3 页

之上才本人感到设想的位置，我们的拍摄意图就可以较好的实现。至于被摄者的表情，那可能就需要更深入的沟通了，也值得进一步探讨。

另外一张拍摄于下山之时，那天独自一人登山，下到半山腰，发现石阶、树木相映成趣，景致不错，遂萌生摄影念头，架好相机，取景时不断寻找合适的摄拍角度及构图，最终尝试斜着构图，让树木看起来有直冲云霄的气势。当时阳光甚好，可以使用较小光圈，以保证足够清晰，然后我飞速跑到位置站定后又突发奇想，在下一刻做一个下山的动作站定，以契合"登山"的主题，或许后发现趣味盎然，静中有动，就赠予你分享。

在信中得知你在老部队生活也是丰富多彩，我友感情甚好，甚慰。特别是作为电影放映员可以在服务同志们的同时锤炼自身技能，也为人生不可多得之乐事，也期待分享更多的照片和故事。

此致，顺颂秋祺！

许宇
1982年9月14日于福州

寄：新疆维吾尔自治区乌鲁木齐市乌鲁木齐县
南山小渠乡村W6619部队 地星3组
何十海（同志）收

福建省福州市仓山区上渡325号 郭乡诚

830063

350007

Dear He Bo,

Your letter arrived a few days ago. It's extremely pleasant to see the two photos that are attached.

"Letters are alive," as the old saying goes, yet I think this is insufficient when it comes to photographs. Despite the importance of words in conveying meanings, they must pass through the processes of thinking and expressing on the writer's side, as well as reading and comprehending on the reader's side, providing room for misunderstandings. Photos, on the other hand, are visual objects. The message is conveyed more clearly from the photographer to the audience, which I believe was the primary impulse for the birth of photography.

I've been thinking about taking more photos at the West Lake lately. So, on an afternoon a few days back, I went to West Lake by myself and took some photos for you. Here's a self-portrait taken at the Gengyi Pavilion, which was constructed during the Five Dynasties.

According to legend, every time Wang Yanjun, Emperor Huizong of Min, his concubine, Jinfeng, and their maids took a boat trip on the lake, they changed their clothes and rested here, hence the name. It becomes one of West Lake's most representative sites now so that numerous photo booths are installed for tourists. In the background, you can also find the Wumen Bridge featured in the last photo I sent you.

The portrait-taking process went smoothly this time, for there was a stone bench at the edge of the lake to use as a reference, making it easy to set up: The framing and focus would not be too off when the camera was stationary and so was the bench's relative position to the camera. On top of that, the camera was set lower to get an ideal composition, and the resulting angle makes me look slightly taller than I am.

There are two more self-portraits I took this spring when

I was at Gu Mountain. They're also attached here for you.

The first one was taken at Yongquan Temple, with the Huilong Pavilion in the background and against the Free Pool. Yongquan Temple is a famous Buddhist temple with a long history. It was founded in 783 AD and has been crowded with visitors ever since. It is a representative site in Fuzhou, and John Thomson also took many photos here when he visited Fuzhou.

The other person in the photo is my friend Su Dewang. He had recently become a new father and thus came here to burn incense for his son's blessing. Su suggested taking a photo together as we were about to leave around noon. I set up the camera, then asked Su to stand against the railing while I fixed the framing, focus, and timer. As intended, I went to stand on Su's right side, and that was how the photo came about.

You've mentioned how to communicate with others in a self-portrait in your last letter. A potential solution, I think, is that they could be considered as a reference for composition. To a point where we could direct their stance and pose as we pleased while imagining ourselves beside them.

Once everything is ready and the timer is set, we simply need to walk to the desired position so that our idea for the shoot could be better realized. Concerning the facial expressions of the participants, this may require some in-depth communication and is also worth investigating further.

The other photo was taken on the way down the mountain. I was hiking alone that day. The stone steps and trees formed a beautiful contrast halfway down. The view was also lovely, so I decided to take this photo. I took out my camera and tried to find a good angle to make the trees appear more vigorous, and eventually shot it diagonally. Since the sunlight

was perfect, a narrower aperture was used to increase sharpness. When I ran to my spot in the photo, I decided on a whim to appear like I was heading down to fit in with the hiking theme. Here is the intriguing result, displaying a mix of movement and stillness, and it's my pleasure to share it with you.

I'm also glad to see you having a good time in the army and getting along with your comrades. Working as a projectionist is also a precious opportunity to serve others and train ourselves. Please keep me posted about your future stories and photos.

Warmly,

Xu Lei
September 14, 1982, Fuzhou

4
四

The Second Letter from He Bo

许雷兄

近日边疆气候不佳，故邮件派送搁置数日，目前收到，拆开看照片挣出，喜。

南方已渐入秋，你俩在西湖边的照片来看温度尚佳。凉鞋衬衣，着实惬意。然我所处的南山地区已寒意渐浓，你可从我附上的两张自拍照片读出几分吧？

先说回照片。西湖照片拍摄地曰更衣亭，此名大

来自何博的第二封信

许雷兄：

近日边疆气候不佳，故邮件派送搁置数日，日前收到，拆开看照片掉出，喜。

南方已渐入秋，从你在西湖边的照片来看，温度尚佳。凉鞋衬衣，着实惬意。然我所处的南山地区已凉意渐浓，你可以从我附上的两张自拍照片读出几分吧？

先说回照片。西湖照片拍摄地曰更衣亭，此名大妙。行文中提及此亭始建于五代时期，平日对历史甚有兴趣，故专门翻阅辞海查阅闽王王延钧之生平。忽作一想，如若五代已有相机，喜好声色之闽王是否亦如我等时常自拍作乐？

鼓山二照令我印象深刻。你与苏德旺之合影让我想到两方面的事。其一，就是我上一封信中提到的自拍时多人调动的安排一事。你谈到合影者可以作为取景构图的参照物，这着实需要除我等摄影师之外的其他人有较强的对照相的理解才行。因为一旦涉及大光圈、长焦距的拍摄时，被摄者须保持相对的静止，这种静止一般将延续到操纵相机的人进入取景范围并摆好姿势之时。

这段时间，我也在继续尝试多人同处一画面中的自拍，发现要想拍清晰所有的人，需要费的口舌真不会少。一张最终呈现出来的相片，前期的人员调动都赶上拍电影了。

给你寄的照片里，有一张便是模仿你鼓山二照中那张单人下山的自拍，只不过我将人数变成了五名，地点也挪到了我们南山营房附近平坦的草地上。也想过模仿你的倾斜构图，还想在画面中让五个人在行进中摆出有趣的动作。然五位战友中有二人姿态始终僵硬，而且倾斜构图无合适支撑点（使用的脚架功能不多），只能放弃，中规中矩使用横幅构图，五人动作也商谈一致后，定为"齐步走"。这种动作在我们军队中是很常见的，但从相片上看还是感觉很微妙。大家都是着便装，且神情轻松。与行军训练相比，虽都是摆布，但状态差异太大了。

新疆景好，我们部队所在的南山地区风景亦然。随信附上的另一张照片也呈现了部队驻地南山地区的景致。我出生生活在四川，刚到部队那些日子深深地迷恋上了这里的风光，没有人为干预的、雄壮的景致。只不过我所希望用相机留存的更多的还是"人"，所以纯粹的风景照片也没有拍下多少。

这张骑马的照片，定义成自拍可能会存在歧义。这是由我架设好相机，各种参数设置调整完毕之后，请战友代劳按下的快门。不过最终也因为逆光，面部都黑掉了。我个人认为，自拍不一定非要局限在"按下快门"这个标准上，我们拍摄电影都有导演，那我们自己"导演"出镜头内的动作以及镜头之外，涉及拍照的其他主要因素的话，其实也应算作我们个人的摄影创作吧。这一点上，我与战友之间有着不同的理解，有的战友认为不按快门就不应算是我拍的。关于作者归谁这个问题倒是无关紧要，也没必要为此伤了战友和气，但确认摄影创作主导者的标准或者范畴，这个还真值得继续探讨。因为我身处边疆，外界新的思想和理念难以入来，故而只能靠与兄交流，聊知一二。

此次赠兄之两张照片均摄于外部公共空间，相对易于把握；接下来我可能尝试室内或较封闭场合进行自拍。留待后面与你分享新进展。

对了，前面提到在看你的鼓山二照时，还有一个问题，便是约翰·汤姆逊其人。弟对西方摄影师知晓不多，敢问此人当下尚在否？其来历如何？为何会在游历福州时拍摄不少照片？愿闻其详，此求提高自己。

最后，有个感想，就是说我在拍摄多人同时出现的摆拍照片时（很多是包含我入镜的自拍），感觉到这种形式以及拍照的氛围跟某些纪念或者见证类的合影（往往是严肃地站立或坐着）以及在个人或小群体空间里的自拍都特别不一样，像这张南山脚下的五人摆拍，它既不是公共场合需要一板一眼，也不像营房里平时得闲自拍那般随性惬意。是不是空间的变换和人群的多少都会对照片中人的状态、表情、姿势产生影响？留作下次探讨吧。

窗外雨停，要去准备晚上的放映了。信件便告一段落。望一切都好，盼复。

何 博
1982年9月24日于乌鲁木齐

妙。行文中提及此亭始陈于五代时期，平日对历史甚有兴趣，故老门翻阅辞海查阅闽王王延钧之生平。忽作一想，如若五代已有相机，喜好声色之闽王是否亦如我等时常自拍作乐？

鼓山二照令我印象深刻。你与苏德旺之合影让我想到西方面部事。其一，就是我上一封信中提到的自拍时多人调剂的安排一事。你谈到合影者可以作为取景构图的参照物，这着实需要除我等摄影师之外的其他人有较强的对照相的理解才行。因为一旦涉及大光圈，长焦距的拍摄时，被摄者须保持相对的静止，这种静止一般将延后操纵相机的人进入取景范围并摆好姿势之时。这段时间，我也在继续尝试多人目处一画面中的自拍，发现要想拍着嘛所有的人，需要费的口舌真不会少。一张最终呈现出来的相片，前期的人员调动都赶上拍电影了。给你寄的

3

照片里，有一张便是模仿你鼓山二照中那张单人下山的自拍，只不过我得人数变成了五名，地点也挪到了我们南山营房附近平坦的草地上。

也想过模仿你的倾斜构图，还想在画面中站五个人在行进中摆出有趣的动作。然而五位战友中有二人姿态始终僵破，且倾斜构图无合适支撑点，使用的脚架功能不多，只能放弃，中规中矩使用横幅构图，五人动作也商定一致后，定为齐步走。这

4

种动作在我们军队中是很常见的，但从相片上看还是感觉很微妙。大家都是着便装，且神情轻松。与行军训练相比，都是摆布，但状态差异太大了。新疆景象好，我们部队所在南山地区风景亦然。随信附上的另一张照片也呈现了部队驻地南山地区的景致。我出生生活在四川，刚到部队那些日子深深地迷恋上了这里的风光，没有人为干预的、雄壮的景致。只不过我所希望用相机留

5

存的更多的还是"人"，所以纯粹的风景照片也没有拍下多少。这张骑马的照片，定义成自拍可能念在歧义。这是由我架设好相机，各种参数设置调整完毕之后，请战友代劳按下的快门。不过最终也因为逆光，面部都黑掉了。我个人认为，自拍不一定非要局限在按下快门这个标准上，我们拍摄电影都有导演，那我们自己"导演"出镜头内的动作以及镜头之外，

6

洗发拍照的其他主要因素的话，其实也应算作我们个人的摄影创作吧。这一点上，我与战友之间有着不同理解，有的战友认为不按快门就不应算是我拍的。关于作者归谁这个问题倒是无关紧要，也没必要为此伤了战友和气，但摄影创作的主导者的确认的一些标准或者范畴，这个还真值得继续探讨。因我身处边疆，外界新的思想和理念难以介来，故而只能靠与兄交流，聊知二一。

此次赠兄之两张照片均摄于外部公共空间，相对易于把握，接下来我们能尝试室内或较封闭场合进行自拍。留待后面与你分享新进展。

对了，前面提到在看你的鼓山二照时，还有一个问题，便是约翰·汤姆逊迪其人。弟对西方摄影师知晓不多，敢问此人当下尚在否？其来历如何？为何会在游历福州时拍摄不少照片？愿闻其详。此求提高自己。最后，有个设想，就是说我在拍摄多人同时出现的摆拍照片（很多时候是包含我人镜的自拍）时，感觉到这种形式以及拍照的氛围跟其他纪念或者见证美的合影往往是严重地站立或坐着以及在个人或小群体空间里的自拍都特别不样，像这张南山脚下的五人摆拍，它既不是心共场合需要一板一眼，也不像营房里平时得闲自拍那般随性惬意。是不是空间的变换和人群的多少都会对照片中人的状态、表情、姿势产生影响？留住下次探讨吧。

窗外雪停，电影准备晚上的放映了，信件使告一段落。望一切都好，盼复。

何博

1982年9月24日于乌鲁木齐

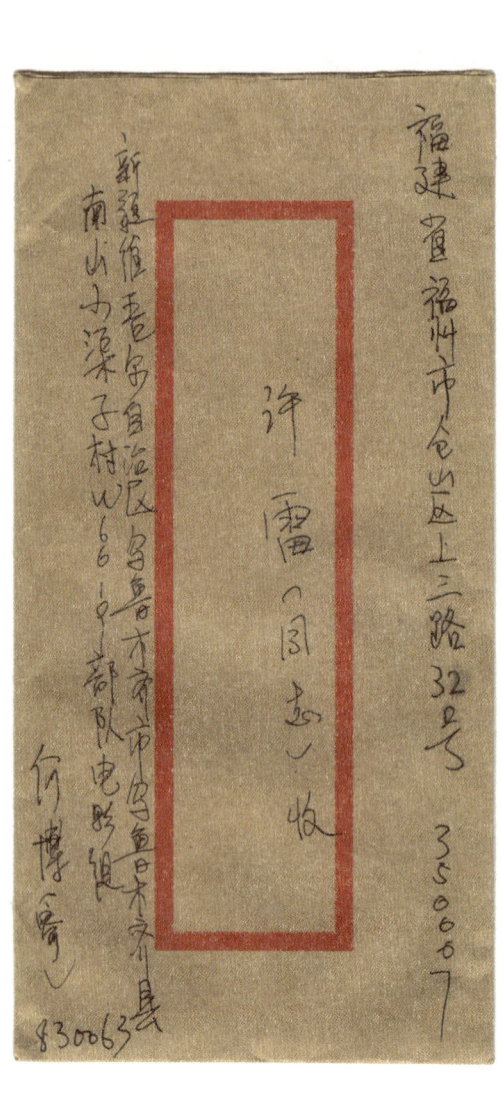

He Bo

Dear Xu Lei,

Your letter finally arrived a few days ago since the mail delivery has recently been delayed due to the bad weather at the border. I was delighted to see your photos fall out as I opened it.

According to your photos taken at the West Lake, it seems that autumn has arrived with lovely weather in the south of China. The sandals and shirt seem to be quite cozy. However, as you can see from the two self-portraits I've attached, it's already getting cold in the Nanshan Pasture where I am now.

Let's get straight into the photos. Gengyi Pavilion, the place where you took your first photo, has a wonderful name. You mentioned that this pavilion was built during the Five Dynasties. As a history enthusiast, I looked up the life of Wang Yanjun, Emperor Huizong of Min, in Cihai. If cameras had been invented during the Five Dynasties, I wonder if he, as a hedonist, would have enjoyed taking self-portraits as much as we do?

The other two photos taken at Gu Mountain have also left a lasting impression on me. Two thoughts came to me when I saw the photo of you and Su Dewang.

One is about the mise-en-scène of the participants. You suggested that they might be considered as a reference for composition, which implies that they, besides the photographer, must also have some solid understanding of photography. But when it comes to shooting with a wide aperture or with a long focal distance, the subject must remain reasonably still, and this stillness will have to last until the photographer enters the frame and is properly posed.

Recently, I've been practicing self-portrait with a group of people and discovered that getting it done properly requires a lot of effort. A group portrait might take the same level of overall planning as a film.

In one of the photos attached, I made a reference to your portrait taken at Gu Mountain, but with more people and in a different setting; there were five of us and we were at a flat grassy area near the barracks at Nanshan. I also considered recreating your diagonal composition and doing some casual poses. However, the two of us were never at ease, and I didn't find a way to support my camera for a similar composition (the tripod we used wasn't that flexible), so I had to drop the idea. Instead, I ended up shooting it horizontally and having everyone do a marching pose in front of the camera, as we had agreed.

This kind of pose can be seen everywhere in the army, but it still appears to be somehow out of place in the photo especially because everyone was dressed casually and seemed quite relaxed. Furthermore, because everything was just staged for photos, our state of mind was completely different than when we were doing serious marching training.

The scenery in Xinjiang is spectacular, and so is the scenery in Nanshan, where our company is based. Another photo attached to this letter captures precisely the view of Nanshan. I was born and raised in Sichuan, so it wasn't a surprise that I fell in love almost immediately with the scenery here during my first few days in the army.

It is truly a majestic place without human intervention. However, I wanted to document more faces with my camera, so I didn't spend much time shooting landscapes. This photo of me on a horse is technically not a self-portrait. Since I asked my comrade to press the shutter button after I had set up the camera and everything else. Besides, the backlighting made my face completely dark in the photo.

Personally, I do not think that the act of pressing the shutter necessarily completes the definition of a self-portrait. Every film has a director, and the same goes for every photo. If we have directed everything from the beginning to the end except pressing the shutter, the output should still be regarded as our work.

My comrades and I think differently on this matter. Some of them insist that I don't have the authorship of it simply because I didn't press the shutter. It makes no difference whether or not I should be regarded as the author in this case, and I have no intention to offend anyone by fighting about it. However, it appears to me that some standard is needed for defining the author of a photo.

As I live at the border, it's not easy for me to keep up with new ideas and trends from the outside world, whereby your letters serve as my window.

The two photos attached this time were all shot in the open air, which is pretty straightforward to manage. Next, I might try taking self-portraits indoors or in a more enclosed environment. I will keep you updated on this.

Speaking of which, your two photos from Gu Mountain got me thinking about John Thomson. As I'm unfamiliar with Western photographers, may I ask as to whether he is still around? What is his background and what made him take so many photos during his time in Fuzhou? I'd like to know more and see what I can learn from him.

My one last thought is about staged group portraits (in which I'm also present). It seems to me that they're different in format and vibe to those souvenir photos (where people generally stand or sit in a serious manner) and those self-portraits taken singly or in a smaller setting. For example, Nanshan, where I shot the group portrait of five people, is a space that is neither as serious as those public areas nor as casual as the barracks during the breaks. Is it possible that the change of space and the size of the crowd had an impact on the mood, expression, and pose of the people captured in portraits?

Let's leave this question for next time.

I have to get ready for tonight's screening now that the rain has stopped. So, I'm closing the letter here.

I hope all is well and I look forward to hearing from you.

Best,

He Bo
September 24, 1982, Urumqi

5
五

The Third Letter from Xu Lei

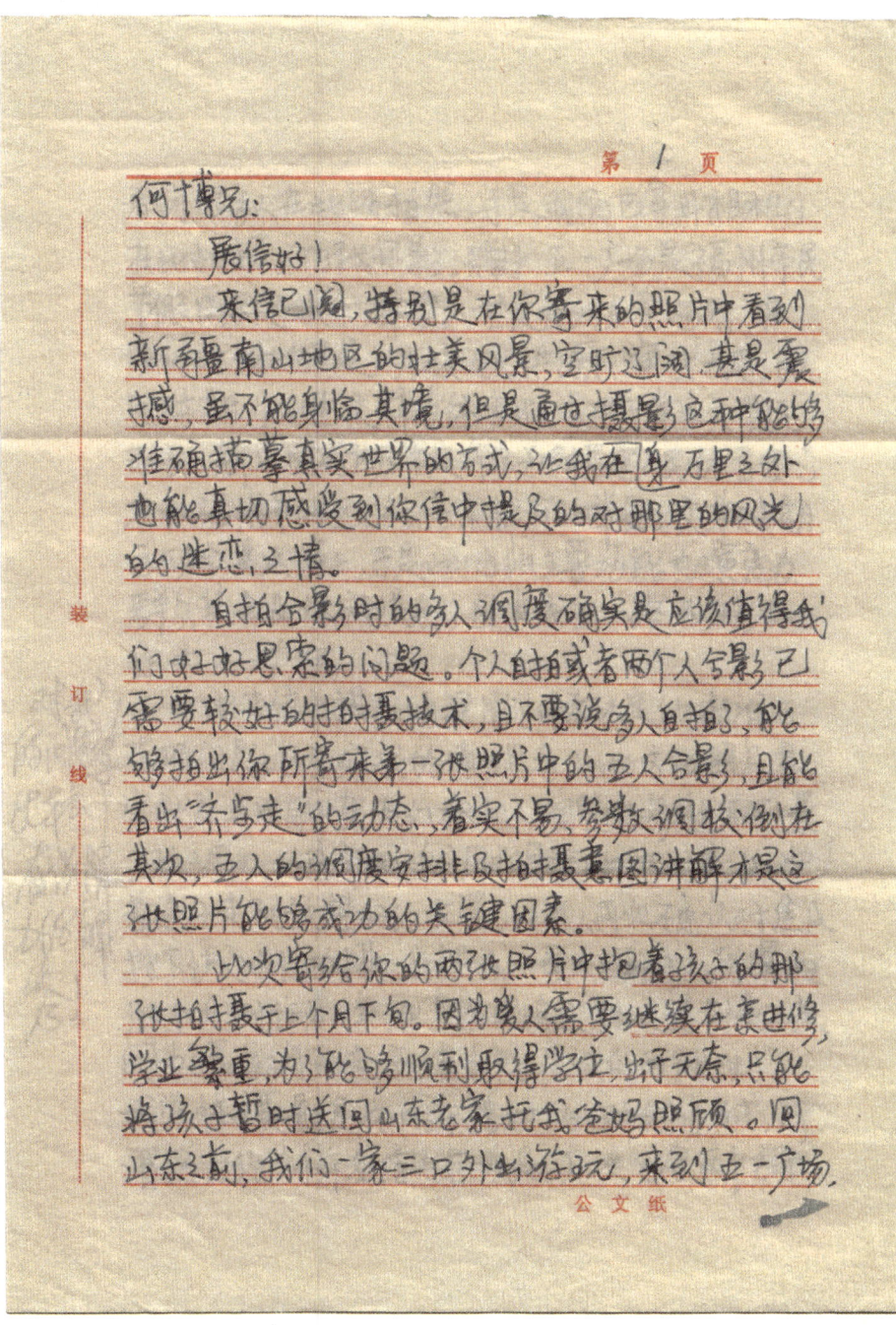

何博兄：

　　展信好！

　　来信已阅，特别是在你寄来的照片中看到新疆南山地区的壮美风景，空旷辽阔，甚是震撼。虽不能身临其境，但是通过摄影这种能够准确描摹真实世界的方式，让我在万里之外也能真切感受到你信中提及的对那里的风光的迷恋之情。

　　自拍合影时的多人调度确实是应该值得我们好好思索的问题。个人自拍或者两个人合影已需要较好的拍摄技术，且不要说多人自拍了，能够拍出你所寄来第一张照片中的五人合影，且能看出"齐步走"的动态，着实不易，参数调校倒在其次，五人的调度安排及拍摄意图讲解才是这张照片能够成功的关键因素。

　　此次寄给你的两张照片中抱着孩子的那张拍摄于上个月下旬。因为妻人需要继续在京也修学业繁重，为了能够顺利取得学位，出于无奈，只能将孩子暂时送回山东老家托我爸妈照顾。回山东之前，我们一家三口外出游玩，来到五一广场。

来自许雷的第三封信

何博兄：

展信好！

来信已阅，特别是在你寄来的照片中看到新疆南山地区的壮美风景，空旷辽阔，甚是震撼。虽不能身临其境，但是通过摄影这种能够准确描摹真实世界的方式，让我身在万里之外也能真切感受到你信中提及的对南山风光的迷恋之情。

自拍合影时的多人调度确实是应该值得我们好好思索的问题。个人自拍或者两人合影已需较好的拍摄技术，且不要说多人自拍了。能够拍出你所寄来第一张照片中的五人合影，且能看出"齐步走"的动态，着实不易。参数调校倒在其次，五人的调度安排及拍摄意图讲解才是这张照片能够成功的关键因素。

此次寄给你的两张照片中抱着孩子的那张拍摄于上个月下旬。因为爱人需要继续在京进修，学业繁重，为了能够顺利取得学位，出于无奈，只能将孩子暂时送回山东老家托我爸妈照顾。回山东之前，我们一家三口外出游玩，来到五一广场，看到很多人在此处拍照，于是我们也拿出相机，在此拍摄了几张留影。

五一广场是福州市民节假日休闲娱乐、举行大型集会的主要场所：在明代时此地已是一片校场，供练兵演武之用；民国时期，此地又辟为体育场，多用于举办大型运动会；新中国成立后被命名为"福建人民体育场"，省和福州市的运动会基本都在此举行；文革时期，运动会基本停止，于是此地的主要功能也演变为群众集会及休闲娱乐。因其在五一路西侧，故称为五一广场。

你来信中提到的照片创作者认定的标准与范畴问题也引发了我的诸多思考：比如这张照片其实就是我用脚架架好相机，调整好参数和取景，大致调好对焦范围，然后指导爱人如何对焦，我抱着孩子走到预想好的位置，让爱人再次确认对焦及按下快门进行拍摄[8]。当然我和爱人之间并无所谓的版权及创作者之争，但是如果涉及别人，特别是如果同为摄影爱好者，就真有产生分歧的可能性了。

我觉得摄影是依附于器材的一种创作方式，所谓照片的创作者，应该包含两个方面，一是熟悉器材使用的技术，二是懂得场面调度安排，即所谓取景构图、画面取舍等艺术化构想，最终谁按下的快门，并不是很重要的。<u>当然，最终按下快门的这个人的取景构图以及对焦的再次确认等也是照片拍摄中不可或缺的</u>[9]，但毕竟是在主导者的指导下进行的，并

8　何博注：对我的问题比较有说服力的解答！

9　编者注：何博在此处划线并标注△符号

第 2 页

看到很多人在此处拍照，于是我们也拿出相机，在此拍持最了几张摄影。赠寺五一广场是福州市民节假日休闲娱乐，举型大型集会的主要场所，在明代时此地已是一片校场，供练兵演武之用。民国时期，此地又辟为体育场，多用于举办大型运动会。新中国成立后被命名为"福建人民体育场"，省和福州市的运动会基本都在此举行。文革时期，运动会基本停止，于是此地的主要功能也演变为群众集会及休闲娱乐。因其在五一路西侧，故欣为五一广场。

你来信中提到的照片创作者认定的标准与范畴等问题也引发我的诸多思考。比如这张照片其实就是我用脚架架好相机，调整好参数和取景，大致调好对焦范围，然后指导爱人如何对焦。我抱着孩子走到预想好的位置，让爱人再次确认对焦及按下快门进行拍摄。当然我和爱人之间并无所谓的版权及创作者之争，但是如果涉及别人，特别是如果同为摄影爱好者，就真有产生分歧的可能性了。我觉得摄影是依附于器材的一种创作形式，所谓照片的创作者，实际应该是应该包含两个方面

对我的问题的比较麻烦的解答！

公文纸

非个人主动性的创造。

这些问题在日常拍摄留影中倒无甚大问题，但如果涉及到参加影赛及报纸刊物刊发之用，倒真要细细研究，特别是如果相机的最终操控者未完全按照主导者的意图拍摄或者比较在意版权归属的话，或许按照署名前后顺序来显示在创作中的主次作用吧。

第二张我个人在五一广场的留影拍摄于前几日。闽地夏秋多台风，前一段台风光顾，无法出门，因妻儿都不在福州，一人待在家中，甚是烦闷。台风过境后，难得见到晴天，故一人出来逛街散心。

走到五一广场，想起前一段还和孩子在此合影，甚是思念，于是萌生在此再留影一张，以做纪念。于是乎选了和前一张照片一样的背景（中间是毛主席雕像的观礼台），但是换了一个方向，拍下此张照片。

上次拍照离观礼台较远，不能看清细节，此次拍摄特意离观礼台近些，你在照片上可以看到上书"毛泽东思想胜利万岁"的展览馆，以及观礼台两边的标语："大海航行靠舵手，干革命靠毛泽东思想"，也可见五一广场真正改造为广场是1969年的文革时期。

上次寄于你的信中有提到约翰·汤姆逊对福州各地的拍摄，因写信匆忙，未及详述，此次就我所知，详述于你。

文革前我在图书馆里浏览过关于此人的英文书籍，所以略知一二，奈何文革十年，外文书籍大量被毁，现今再想去查阅相关资料，比之文革之前反而更加困难。约翰·汤姆逊是英国摄影师，晚清时进入中国多个城市并进行了大规模拍摄，此时应早已不在人世。福州作为第一次鸦片战争之后中国开风气之先的五口通商城市之一，摄影术得以较早传入，所以约翰·汤姆逊能够较便利地进入福州且拍摄了大量的人物和景物，比如鼓山、YUAN-FU寺（暂未考证在何处）等。其所用摄影法为当时流行的湿版法，相较于今日之相机，器材笨重，且程序繁琐，需当场制作玻璃底版，拍摄后当场显影。

当时中国封建思想严重，对"洋人"抵触情绪较大，且误信拍照可摄人灵魂。然而[10]约翰·汤姆逊凭借良好的沟通技巧，拍摄了大量中国人早期的肖像及景物，实属不易。当时的旧中国还几乎没人掌握摄影术之时，他给我们留下了很多珍贵的影像，确实值得敬佩。如有机会，我会继续查找资料，探访当年约翰·汤姆逊在福州拍摄过的地方，拍摄留影后寄于你分享。

关于你最后所提的拍摄形式、空间变换和人数多少等会对照片中之人产生影响的问题，我想这肯定是会有的，但是具体如何影响，待我们自拍或者各种类型的拍摄实践多了之后，会有更多的想法可以交流吧。

信写至此，已到上课时间，期待今后更多深入交流。
祝好！盼复。

许　雷
1982年10月3日于榕城

10　编者注：此处原文为"但是"

第 3 页

一是熟悉器材使用的技术；二是懂得场面调度安排，即所谓取景构图、画面取舍等艺术化构想。最终谁按下的快门并不是很重要的。当然最终按下快门的这个人的取景构图以及对焦的再次确认等也是照片拍摄中不可或缺的，但毕竟是在主导者的指导下进行的，并非个人主动性的创造。这些问题在日常拍摄留影中倒无甚大问题，但如果涉及到参加影赛及报纸刊物刊发之用，倒真要细心研究。特别是如果相机的最终操控者未完全按照主导者的意图拍摄或者比较在意版权归属的话，或许按照署名前后顺序来显示在创作中的主次作用吧。

第三张我个人在玉一广场的留影拍摄于前几日，闽地夏秋多台风，前一段台风光顾，无法出门，因妻儿都不在福州，一人待在家中，甚是烦闷，台风过境后，难得见到晴天，故一人出来逛街散心，走到玉一广场，想起前一段还和孩子在此合影，甚是思念，于是萌生在此再留影一张，以作纪念。于是乎找了和前一张照片一样的背景（中间是毛主席画像的观礼台），但是换了一个方向，拍下此张也

公文纸

第 4 页

照片。上次拍照离观礼台较远，不能看清细节，比次拍摄特意离观礼台近些，你在照片上可以看到上书"毛泽东思想胜利万岁"的展览馆，以及观礼台两边的标语："大海航行靠舵手，干革命靠毛泽东思想。"也可见五一广场真正改造为广场是兴建于1969年的文革时期。

上次寄于您的信中有提到约翰·汤姆逊对福州各地的拍摄，因写信匆忙，未及详述，此次就我所知，详述于您。文革前我在图书馆里浏览过关于此人的英文书籍，所以略知一二，奈何文革十年，外文书籍大量被毁，现今再想去查阅相关资料，比之文革之前反而更加困难。约翰·汤姆逊是英国摄影师，晚清时其入中国多个城市并进行了大规模拍摄，此时应早已不在人世。福州作为第一次鸦片战争后中国开风气之先的五口通商城市之一，摄影术得以较早传入，所以约翰·汤姆逊能够较为方便的出入福州且拍摄了大量的人性方和景物，比如鼓山，YUAN-FU寺（暂未考证在何处）等。其所用摄影法为当时流行的湿版法，相较于今日之相机，器材笨重且程序繁琐，需当场制作玻璃底版，拍摄拍后当场显影

公文纸

且当时中国封建思想严重，对"洋人"抵触情绪较大，且迷信拍照可摄人灵魂。但约翰·汤姆逊凭借良好的沟通技巧，拍摄了大量中国人早期的肖像及景物，实属不易。当时的旧中国还没几个人掌握摄影术之时，他给我们留下了很多珍贵的影像，确实值得敬佩。如有机会，我会继续查找资料，探访当年约翰·汤姆逊在福州拍摄过的地方，拍摄照影后寄予你分享。

关于你最后所提的拍摄形式、空间变换和数多少等会对照片中人产生影响的问题，我想这肯定是会有的，但是具体如何影响，待我们自己或者各种类型的拍摄实践多了之后，会有更多的想法可以交流吧。信鸟引妙，已到上课时间，期待今后更多洋的交流。祝好！盼复。

郑雷
1982年10月3日于榕城

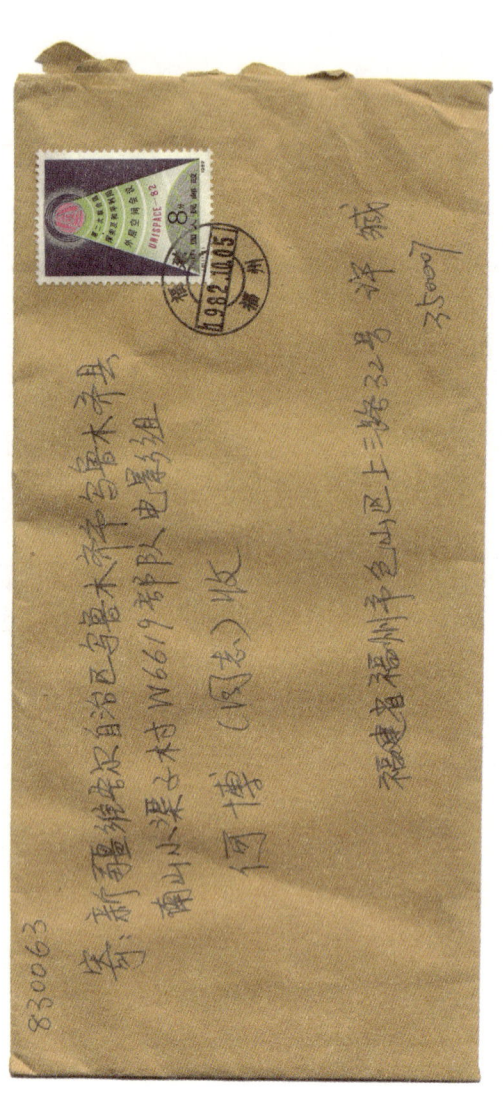

寄：新疆维吾尔自治区乌鲁木齐市
南山小渠子村W6619部队政治部3组
何博（风志）收

830063

福建省福州市鼓山区上岐32号 许葴

350007

71 Xu Lei → He Bo

Dear He Bo,

Your letter is well appreciated. The photos of the scenery in Nanshan Pasture are especially impressive. Even though I'm thousands of miles away, I could still genuinely relate to your love for the place through photography, a medium that is capable of depicting reality objectively.

The mise-en-scène for a group portrait is something we need to dig into. A good self-portrait with oneself or with another person already requires a lot of experience, let alone a group portrait with more people involved. Capturing the marching vibe in that photo of five people seems to be a real challenge. The success of this photo shoot lies in the coordination of all parties and the delivery of the photographer's idea besides all the technical matters.

One of the photos attached to this letter was shot with my son late last month. Since my wife will soon be off to Beijing to continue her studies and in order to make way for that, we have no alternative but to send our son back to my hometown in Shandong to be with my parents. Before we left for Shandong, the three of us had a family day at Fuzhou Wuyi Square. Many people were taking photos there and so were we.

Wuyi Square is the main gathering spot for the Fuzhou people: During the Ming Dynasty, it served as a military training ground; when it came to the Republic of China, it was used as a stadium, primarily for large-scale sport events; after the founding of the new China, it was named "Fujian People's

Stadium," and almost all sport events in Fujian Province and Fuzhou City were held here; but since the Cultural Revolution, almost all sport events were suspended, and it was repurposed as a place for gatherings till now. The name is taken from its location, which is at the west of Wuyi Road.

It seems appropriate now to take this photo with my son as an example to address what you said about the standard of defining the author, which really sparked a lot of thoughts in me. It was "taken" by my wife as I instructed her to focus after I set up the camera in terms of framing and a rough focus range. Then I asked her to press the shutter once I was ready at my ideal location with my son in my arms. Of course, my wife and I would never have an authorship issue. However, in other cases, especially if I was among other photographers, the story may be different.

Photography, in my opinion, is an equipment-based artistic creation. The author of a photographic work should be accountable for the following two things: The first is equipment familiarity, and the second is the coordination of mise-en-scène, which includes framing, composition, and other aesthetic decisions. The very act of pressing the shutter button is not the most important. Apparently, everything should be double-checked before the final act. But since it's all guided by the "director," the act of pressing the button does not take part in the creative process.

In most cases, authorship is not an issue in souvenir photos. However, it may cause serious problems when it comes to photo competitions and publishing, especially if the person who presses the shutter button does not follow all the intentions of the "director" or if the person is concerned about authorship. In this case, perhaps it is a good way to resolve the problem with the order of authors according to their contributions.

The second photo of me at Wuyi Square was taken a few days ago. Typhoons are common in Fujian during the summer and autumn. Since my wife and son were not here at the time, I was trapped alone at home due to the recent typhoon. As soon as the first sunny day arrived, I went out for a walk to Wuyi Square.

The place made me feel nostalgic as I thought about the other photo with my son taken before he left, so I decided to take another one as a keepsake. I used the same background as last time (the reviewing stand with a Chairman Mao's statue in the middle) but from another side.

Last time we were far from the reviewing stand, so the photo didn't capture many details. This time I went closer and took another one in which you may see the exhibition hall titled "Long live the victory of Maoism" and the slogan on both sides,

"Navigation depends on the helmsman. Revolution depends on Chairman Mao." Thus, Wuyi Square functioning as a place for gathering is apparently a result of the Cultural Revolution in 1969.

I was in a rush to write to you last time, so I only mentioned John Thomson and his trip to Fuzhou very briefly. Let me go into more details this time.

I read about him in some English books from the library before the Cultural Revolution, and that's how I learned about him. However, after ten years of the Cultural Revolution many foreign language books were destroyed. They are thus less accessible than before.

John Thomson, a British photographer who traveled to numerous cities in China and took many photos during the late Qing Dynasty, passed away a long time ago. As photography was first introduced to Fuzhou, one of China's first five trade ports after the First Opium War, the port's opening up allowed John Thomson to freely access the city to photograph the local scenery and people, such as Gu Mountain and the YUAN-FU Temple (the location is not yet confirmed), etc.

Technically, he employed the Collodion process, which was popular at the time. The equipment used for this process is much more cumbersome and complicated to manage compared to modern ones. It requires the glass plate to be coated, sensitized, exposed, and developed within a short span of time.

Many people in China were unfriendly to foreigners at that time because of the feudal ideas prevalent caused by the closed-door policy. There's also the sorcery scare about cameras stealing souls to form photos. John Thomson, on the other hand, was able to benefit from a certain amount of freedom owing to his outstanding communication skills.

He left us many photographic archives that are truly precious at a time when nearly no one in old China had mastered the technique of photography. If I get the chance, I will keep looking into him and visit more places where he photographed in Fuzhou to share with you.

In response to your last question, I believe there is no doubt that the change in space and the number of participants will affect the final result. But how it's affected and to what extent is something we need to figure out till we have more experience with self-portraits or other types of photography.

It's almost time for my class so I have to stop here. I can't wait to continue this conversation with you.

Talk soon,

Xu Lei
October 3, 1982, Fuzhou

6
六

The Third Letter from He Bo

许雷兄：

前几日从广播中听闻福建被台风侵袭，后从你的来信中颇知一些事。甚挂，望兄及家人无恙。又观兄台风后自拍，闲情依然，故知无碍。

收到你附上的两张照片，加上你信中提到的摄子按快门，你来指导构建的例子，让我对于自拍照片作者的界定问题有了较之前更清楚的认识。尤其，是你摄到的场面调度，此举一如电影导演，和舞台演出指导

来自何博的第三封信

许雷兄：

前几日从广播中听闻福建被台风侵袭，后从你的来信中确知以事。甚挂，望兄及家人无恙。又观兄台风后自拍，闲情依然，故知无碍。

收到你附上的两张照片，加上你信中提到的嫂子按快门，你来指导构建的例子，让我对于自拍照片作者的界定问题有了较之前更清楚的认识。尤其是你提到的场面调度，此举一如电影导演和舞台演出指导者在集体工作中所做的一样。我们设置好相机，再走到镜头前面对相机，只是多了一重身份：被摄者或者表演者。

触发快门的可以是快门线，也可以是其他的人。这在理论上是没有问题的。但在我的实际拍摄中，体会到了一个问题，这问题也就是你在信中说到的："当然，最终按下快门的这个人的取景构图以及对焦的再次确认等，也是照片拍摄中不可或缺的"，这一点其实相当重要。一切调整好之后，换过去按快门的人最好是相对了解拍照的人。别的不说，有的战友在我之前的自拍导演[11]实验里，按快门时没有扶好相机，造成了最后出片效果模糊，着实遗憾。

这一问题是我这次寄给你的两张照片涉及的主要话题。这两张都是舞台照，是我们电影组应上级要求，拍摄的宣传照中的两张。因我在连队中不光在电影组服务，还同时参与连队的舞蹈表演及主持报幕工作，故而亦有出镜。这也给了我实践在照度较低的室内环境中，通过人工布光（当然也是舞台表演本身要求的布光方式）来进行自拍的机会。

你看到的我与另外五名战友在舞台上叉腰的照片就专门是为了宣传而进行的摆拍任务，而非现场演出。不过，我们六人的服装和姿势都来自我们常演的一出剧目《谁偷了巴依家的西瓜？》。其实在拍照时，大家应该保持不动，不过，静止的摆拍让有的战友感到不自然，表情亦僵硬，当时帮忙按快门的战友焦钢（之前的信里提到过他，此兄与我在长城上的合照业已赠予你）建议大家不妨按照剧中的情节动起来，且幅度不要过大，如此呈现出稍微自然一些的状态。我无异议，其他战友亦赞同，最右边的战友王大壮最为投入，欣而舞动，最终在照片里也显得较为模糊。

成品虽不完美，但不妨碍这场拍摄变得有趣，或者说更有意义。所以谈到这，我想到了宣传照片是否真的必须一板一眼地地设计，容不得一丁点儿的发挥？

至少从这张照片后来收到的反馈来看，是积极的。其他连队的战友中，有许多人都找到我们反映，说这种不看镜头的、感觉像是抓拍的照片比原先那些固定模式的宣传照有意思。有的战友还不知道这张照片确实不是抓拍而来。这些反馈让我着实开心了一会儿。

另一张照片亦为摆拍，不过只有我一人是"演员"。此照片实为捡漏完成之作。那日连队活动，我被派为主持人，想着既然需要拍摄表现工作的宣传照，便把相机和脚架一同拿去了现场。拍摄是同彩排一同进行的，你可以看到我的身后站着准备进行合唱排练的领导和首长们，他们里的一部分早已退伍，这次是专程被请回来参加演出。我便在开演前这一相对宽松的时间段里完成了三张自拍。这张赠予你的版本同时也作为宣传照之一贴在了公告栏里。

此番挑选这两张舞台上的照片赠你，也是拜兄照片赐以灵感。你的两张同一地点不同时间、不同被摄者的影像提醒我也选择拍摄场所相同的照片。甚者，你的照片让我产生了一些新的想法：如若经年之后，请原先在某地拍摄过一张照片的人，再到故地拍一张照片，会不会比较有意义？再如果，被拍的人是我们自己，心中会否更加感慨？试想，如果这两张五一广场自拍留念的间隔不是三五天，而是十年二十年，如果多年后不是你抱着你的孩子，而是与之并肩站在镜头前，将之前与之后的照片放在一起，将是何种感受？行笔至此，期待之心竟然异常迫切。但愿多年之后能将此愿景付诸实践。

末了，感谢雷兄对于约翰·汤姆逊的介绍。一座城市能够在上个世纪就被如此系统地拍摄、记录，真是一件好事。也羡慕雷兄在大学丰富的资源，图书馆里想必与摄影相关的资料亦不少，相比之下，我在边疆连队里，能看到的相关资料实在是太缺乏了。只希望今后复员回乡，能去一座大城市，多长点学识。

遥祝安康，问嫂子、小侄好！盼复。

另，此次信封取到后，发现背后贴一张纸条，书"已查，无异"，甚为不解。

何 博

八二年十月于乌鲁木齐

---

11 编者注：何博在"自拍"与"导演"之间加入对调号

者在集体工作中所做的一样，我们设置好相机之再走到镜头前再将相机之是复了重复有伤。被摄者或者表演者。触发快门的可以是快门线也可以是其他的人。这在理论上是没有问题的。但在我的实际拍摄中，体会到了一个问题，这问题也就是你在信中说到的"当然，最后，按下快门的这个人的取景构图以及对焦的再次确认等也是照片拍摄中不可或缺的。"这一点尤其是相当重要。一切调整好之后，换过去按快门的人最好是相要对了解拍照的人。别的不说，有的战友在我之前的自拍寺渡实验里，按快门时没抖好相机，造成了最左出片效果模糊，着实遗憾。这一问题是我这次寄给你的两张照片涉及的主题: 这两张都是舞台照，是我们电影组应上级要求拍摄的宣传照中的两张，因我在连队中不光在电影组中服务，还同时参与连队的舞蹈表演及主持报幕工作，故而亦有出镜，这也给了我实战在照废较低

3

的室内环境中，通过人工布光（闪灯）也是舞台表演本身需要的布光方式）进行自拍的机会。你看到的我会另外叫上战友在舞台上又腰的照片，就专门是为了宣传而的摆拍任务，非现场演出。不过，我们六人的服装和姿势乃都来自我们排演的一出剧目《谁偷了巴依家的西瓜？》。其实在拍照时，大家应该保持不动，不过，静止的摆拍让有的战友感到不自然，表情、亦僵硬，当时帮忙按快门的战友焦铜之前的信里提到过他，党与我在长城上的合照（业已赠予你）建议大家不妨按照剧中的情节动起来，且幅度不要过大，如此主现出稍微自然一些的状态。我无异议，其他战友亦赞同，最右边的战友王大治最为投入，欣而舞动最怂，在照片里显得最为模糊。成品虽不完美，但不妨碍这场拍摄变得有趣，或者说更有意义，所以谈到这，我想到了官俊照片是否真的挨领一板一眼地设计，密不得一丁点儿的发挥？至少从这张照片看来

5

收到的反馈来看,是积极的。其他连队的战友中,有许多人都找到我们反映,说这种不看镜头的感觉像是抓拍的照片比原先那些固定模式的宣传照有意思。有的战友还不知道这张照片确实不是抓拍而来。这些反馈让我着实开心了一会儿。

另一张照片亦为摆拍,不过只有我一人是演员。此照实为拾漏完成之作。那日连队活动,我被派为主持人,想着既然需要拍摄表现工作的宣传照,便把相机和脚架一同拿去了现场，拍摄足同彩排一同进行的，你可以看到我的身后站着准备进行合唱排练的领导和首长们，他们里的一部份早已退位，这次是专程邀请回来参加演出。我便在开演前这一相对宽松的时间段里完成了三张自拍。这张赠予你的版本同时也作为宣传照（之一）贴在了公告栏里。

此番挑选这两张舞台上的照片赠你，也是

7

拜兄照片赐以灵感。你的两张同一地点不同时间、不同被摄者的影像提醒我也选择拍摄场所相同的照片。甚者，你的照片让我产生了一些新的想法：

如若经年之后，请原先在某地拍摄过一张照片的人，再到故地相同场所拍一张照片，会不会比较有意义？再如果，被拍的人是我们自己，心中会否更加感慨？试想，如果这两张五一广场自拍留念的间隔不是三五天，而是十年二十年，如果多年

8

后不是你抱着你的孩子，而是与之并肩站在镜头前，将之前与之后的照片放在一起，将是何种感受？行笔至此，期待之心竟异常迫切。但愿多年之后能将因此愿景付诸实践。

末了，感谢雷兄对于伯翰·汤姆迪的介绍，一座城市能够在上个世纪就被如此系统地拍摄记录真是一件好事。也羡慕雷兄在大学丰富的资源，图书馆里想必与摄影相关的资料亦不少，相比之下,我在边远连队里,能看到的相关资料实在是太缺乏了,以希望今后复员回乡,能去大城市,多长点学识。

遥祝安康,问嫂子、小侄好!盼复。

另,此次信封取到后,发现背后贴一张条,书"邓查,无异",甚为不解。

何博

八二年七月于昌吉末字井

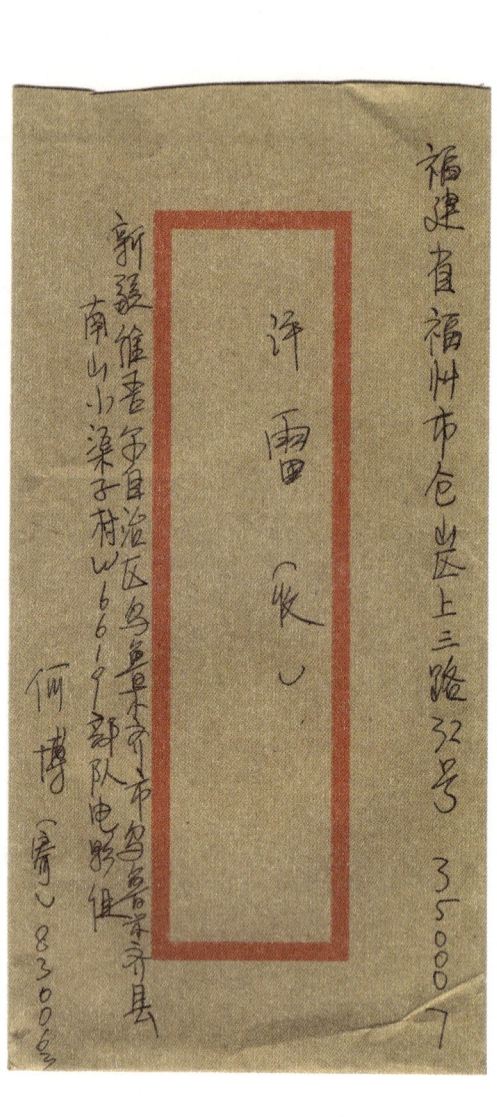

91 Xu Lei — He Bo

Dear Xu Lei,

I heard on the radio a few days ago that Fujian had been hit by a typhoon, which you confirmed in your letter. My thoughts are with you and your family. Thankfully, your self-portrait post-typhoon seems to suggest you're doing well.

The two photos you sent and the story of your collaboration with your wife helped me better understand the nuances in defining the authorship of a photo. I'm particularly interested in what you said about mise-en-scène, which precisely mirrors what a film director or a stage director does in their collaborative work. We set up the camera and then enter the frame, but this time with a new role: subject or performer.

The shutter can be activated by a cable release or by another person, which is fine in theory. In my experience, however, I constantly run into the same situation, which you also mentioned in your letter: "Apparently, everything should be double-checked before the final act." This is quite important.

After everything has been set up, the person who will press the shutter button should ideally be someone with some basic understanding of photography. Apart from anything else, it's such a pity that one of the photographs from my self-portrait test is extremely blurry only because my comrade didn't hold the camera steady while pressing the shutter.

The two photos I am sending you this time both touch upon this issue. They are both staged just like the publicity photos that our film crew took at the request of our superiors. In addition to being a part of the film crew, I also serve as a host for some performances and participate in the company's dance shows, which explains my presence in the photos.

Fortunately, my multiple roles in the company also give me the chance to practice taking self-portraits in a low-light indoor setting with artificial lighting, which is used for stage performances. The photo of me on stage with five other comrades, arms akimbo, was not taken during a live performance but was rather staged. The costumes and poses of all six of us are from a play called "Who Stole the Watermelon from the Master," which we perform frequently. We were supposed to stand still for the photo, but some of my comrades found it unnatural to hold a still pose in front of the camera, and their unease was clearly shown on their faces. To solve this problem, Jiao Gang (I've sent you a photo of him and me on the Great Wall) suggested that we make some small movements as if we were performing the play to help us relax. We all found that an excellent idea. The one on the far right, Wang Dazhuang, was the most engaged and therefore out of focus in the photo.

Even though the final result isn't perfect, I still find the process quite interesting and meaningful. In that vein, I wonder, do publicity photos have to be meticulously arranged, leaving no room for creativity?

People seem to like this photo, at least based on their feedback. Many comrades from other companies told us that this type of photograph, which seems like a snapshot, is more interesting than traditional publicity shots. Some of them had no idea the photo was not a snapshot, but still, their reaction made me very pleased.

The other photo, in which I am the only performer, is also staged. It came to me by pure chance. That day, I was appointed to be the host of a company event. I assumed I'd need to take some publicity shots, so I brought my camera and tripod with me. The photo was taken during the choir rehearsal, so the leaders can be seen standing behind me. Some of them had already been released from the army and were invited back for the performance. With the extra time before the performance began, I was able to finish three self-portraits. This one was also displayed on the bulletin board.

I was inspired by your last photos to send you these two staged photos of mine. Your works in the same location with different subjects at different times really intrigued me to try something similar.

They even gave me some new ideas: Would it be more interesting if we asked someone who had taken a photo in a certain location to take another shot in that same location years later? Are we going to feel even more strongly about it if we were the person in the photo? Imagine how you would feel if these two self-portraits at Wuyi Square were taken not three or five days apart, but ten or twenty years apart, and if years later instead of you holding your son in your arms, you two were standing side by side in front of the camera. What would your reaction be if you saw these before and after photos together? As I'm writing it, I'm already excited about this idea. I hope it will be realized in the future.

Lastly, many thanks for the information about John Thomson. It's incredible that a city has been photographed and documented so carefully in the last century. I also envy you for the wealth of resources available at the university. I'm sure the library has plenty of photography-related material.

In comparison, the materials within my reach at the border are extremely limited. I just hope that when I return to my hometown after demobilization, I will be able to live in a big city and expand my knowledge with better resources.

Take care of yourself and your family. I eagerly await your response.

Warm wishes,

He Bo
October 1982, Urumqi

P.S. When I received your letter this time, the note on the back of envelope that marked "checked, no problem" really perplexed me.

7
七

The Fourth Letter from Xu Lei

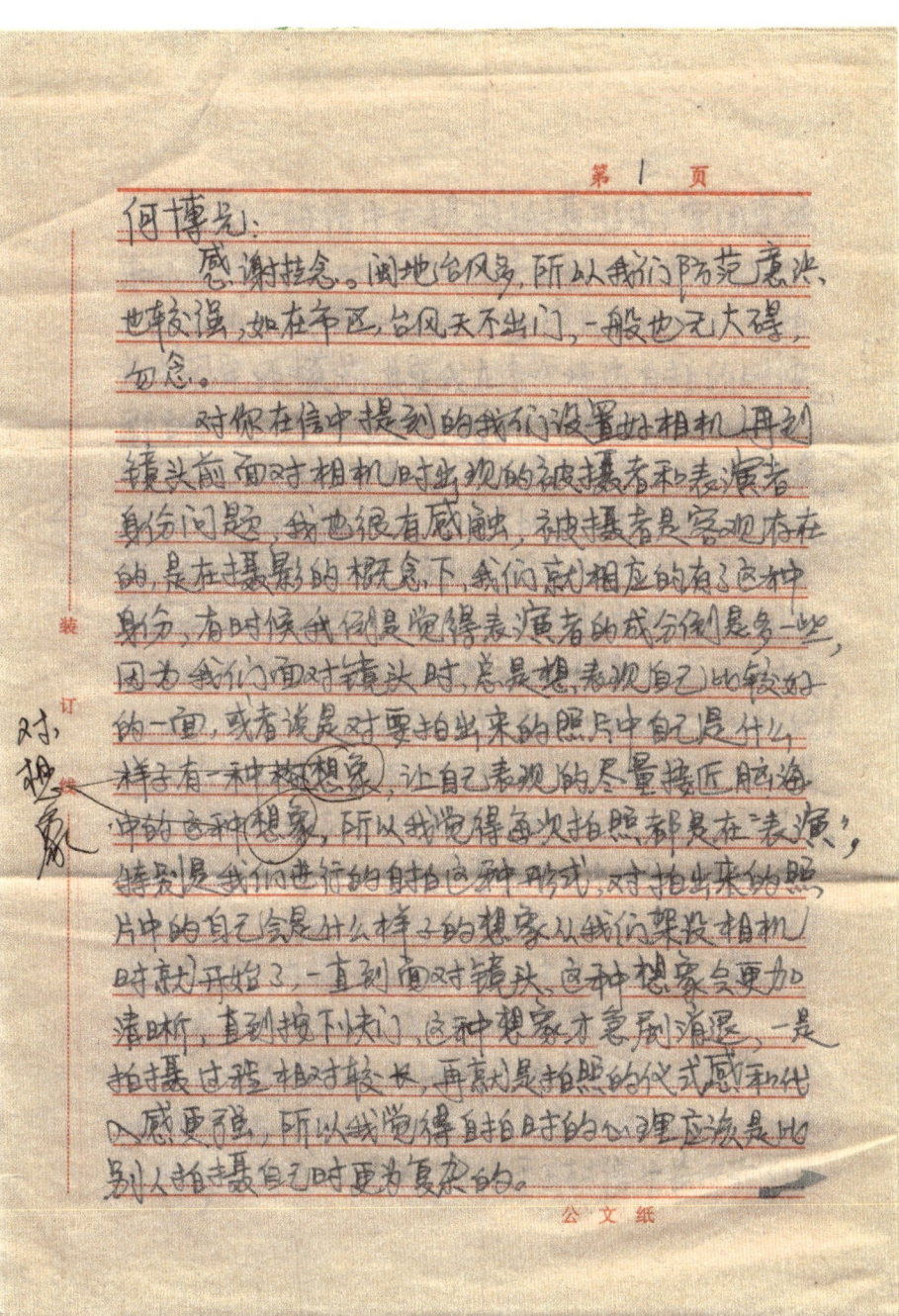

第 1 页

何博兄：

感谢挂念。闽地台风多，所以我们防范意识也较强，如在市区，台风天不出门，一般也无大碍，勿念。

对你在信中提到的我们设置好相机，再到镜头前面对相机时出现的被摄者和表演者身份问题，我也很有感触。被摄者是客观存在的，是在摄影的概念下，我们就相应的有了这种身份。有时候我们总觉得表演者的成分倒是多一些，因为我们面对镜头时，总是想表现自己比较好的一面，或者说是对要拍出来的照片中自己是什么样子有一种构想（想象），让自己表现的尽量接近脑海中的这种想象，所以我觉得每次拍照都是在"表演"，特别是我们进行的自拍这种形式，对拍出来的照片中的自己会是什么样子的想象从我们架设相机时就开始了，一直到面对镜头，这种想象会更加清晰，直到按下快门，这种想象才急剧消退。一是拍摄过程相对较长，再就是拍照的仪式感和代入感更强。所以我觉得自拍时的心理应该是比别人拍摄自己时更为复杂的。

对，想象

公 文 纸

来自许雷的第四封信

何博兄：

感谢挂念。闽地台风多，所以我们防范意识也较强，如在市区，台风天不出门，一般也无大碍，勿念。

对你信中提到的我们设置好相机再到镜头前面对相机时出现的被摄者和表演者身份问题，我也很有感触。

被摄者是客观存在的，是在摄影的概念下，我们就相应地有了这种身份。有时候我倒是觉得表演者的成分多一些，因为我们面对镜头时，总是想表现自己比较好的一面，或者说是对要拍出来的照片中自己是什么样子有一种想象，让自己表现得尽量接近脑海中的这种想象[12]。所以我觉得每次拍照都是在"表演"，特别是我们进行的自拍这种形式，对拍出来的照片中的自己会是什么样子的想象从我们架设相机时就开始了，一直到面对镜头，这种想象会更加清晰，一直到按下快门，这种想象才急剧消退。

一是拍摄过程相对较长，再就是拍照的仪式感和代入感更强，所以我觉得自拍时的心理应该是比别人拍摄自己时更为复杂的。

你前一封信中也提到拍摄形式、空间变换和人数多少等会对照片中之人产生影响，就我自己之前还有这次寄给你的这些照片来说吧：自拍没有固定的模式，其实我在各个地方自拍的时候都自觉不自觉地按照自己平常所见到的旅游纪念照的方式来拍，可以说是自觉不自觉地模仿他们的拍摄方式，因为看得多了，总会留下一些印象，有些固有模式[13]。特别是我在将底片交于照相馆冲印的时候，有时也会交代其按照他们固有的加工方式加上以文字标注的拍摄地点和时间，所以这些照片，很多在形式上都和平时的旅游纪念照有些相似。但是细看照片之上我的表情，又不是非常严肃和呆板，一般都是比较轻松愉悦的表情，或许当时我的内心也是在享受这种自导自演的的拍摄吧，已经沉浸其中，表情就自然流露了。反观旅游留念，在摄影师指挥下，快速站定，咔嚓一下，表情或严肃或呆板，有时甚至是疑惑。

此次寄于你的两张照片也是前几日拍摄的，拍摄于福州于山，此景区涵盖范围较大，其中也有很多有特色的景点。于山位于上封信寄于你的照片中的五一广场的北侧[14]（其实就是在毛主席塑像及纪念馆的后面）。

我此次主要选择了于山西麓定光寺（也称白塔寺）内较有特色的定光塔（俗称白塔）为背景，并且选择了不同地点和角度的两张照片，如果你细看一下我上封信中寄于你的两张照片，在毛主席塑像的后面都可以看到白塔的身影[15]。

定光塔全名报恩定光多宝塔，为福州"三山两塔"（乌山、于山、屏山和乌塔、白塔）地标之一，是闽王王审知（也就是曾给你的信中提到的闽王王延钧的父亲，为闽国的建立者）为其父母荐福，于唐天佑元年（公元904年）建造，次年才在塔南建定光寺。传说在挖塔基时，发现一颗光芒四射的宝珠，故名定光塔。明嘉靖十三年（1534年），塔被雷而毁。嘉靖二十七年（1548年）重建后，仅有原塔之半的高度，共七层，塔身用白灰粉刷，故称白塔。

第一张照片拍摄于早晨刚到定光寺之际。近几日福州也开始降温，所以晨起要穿外套了。我在寺内一边游览，一边寻找合适的拍摄地点，经过天王殿和大雄宝殿，当来到法雨堂时，发现白塔可清晰映入眼帘，于是选取合适的角度，取景构图。因法雨堂前空地较窄，所以只能用仰拍，这样也正好将白塔完整地收入镜头了。我此次是以照片左侧的树木作为参照，设置好相机后我就靠着树枝站到了右边，现在看来，效果还算满意吧。

拍完这张照片后继续游览，发现寺内可游览的地方甚多，不知不觉已到午间，天气变热，遂除去外套在榕寿岩旁的石凳休息，发现在此处看去，白塔也清晰可见，且正好旁边有古榕相衬，景致甚好，于是趁休息之际不断琢磨如何取景构图。发现从我所处的位置望向白塔，正好有一石栏杆挡住白塔底部，于是想着拍照时干脆舍弃白塔底部，我坐在石栏杆上，只取石栏以上部分，而且水平的石栏还可以作为构图时的一个很好的参照。于是拍摄时将取景器底线和石栏的上沿水平对齐，调好焦，定好时间，我坐到石栏上进行了拍摄。

因使用的是旁轴相机，当时疏忽了视差，所以部分石栏最终还是呈现在了照片中。不过我想这种稍微有点"意外[16]"的效果倒是让我感觉更好，试想，如果真像我预想的那样完全舍弃石栏，最终我是一种坐姿的"漂浮"状态，无所依靠，倒会显得怪异。我想这也是摄影总能给我们带来惊喜的原因吧。我们构建想象，用心拍摄，但总要等一阵子，冲洗后拿到照片，才能真正看到照片拍摄的效果。先不管效果是好是坏，只是

---

12 何博注：对，想象

13 编者注：何博在此处划线并标注△符号

14 编者注：此处原文为"其位于上封信中寄于你的照片中的拍摄地点五一广场的北侧"

15 编者注：何博在此处划线并标注"找找看"

16 编者注：何博在此处圈出"意外"二字并标注√符号

第 2 页

你前一封信中也提到拍摄形式、空间变换和人数多少等会对照片中人产生影响，就我自己之前还有这次寄给你的这些照片来说吧，自拍没有固定的模式。其实我在各个地方自拍的时候，都自觉不自觉地以拍照、或自己用眼所见到的旅游留念照的方式来拍。可以说是自觉不自觉地模仿他们的拍摄方式，因为看的多了，总会留下一些印象，有些固有模式。特别是我在将底片交于照相馆冲印的时候，有时也会交代其按照他们固有的加工方式加上以文字标注的拍摄地点和日时间，所以这些照片，很多在形式上都和平时的旅游纪念照有些相似，但是细看照片之上我的表情，又不是非常平素和呆板，一般都是比较轻松愉悦的表情，或许当时我的内心也是在享受这种自导自演的拍摄吧，已经沉浸其中，表情就自然流露了。反观旅游留念，在摄影师指挥下，快速站定，咔嚓一下，表情或平素或呆板，有时甚至疑惑。

此次寄于你的两张照片也是前几日拍摄的，拍摄于福州于山，此景区涵盖范围较大，其中也有很多有特色的景点，其住于上封信中寄于你的

公 文 纸

拿到照片的那一刻，我们的内心就充满了期待的喜悦。

你信中提到羡慕我的工作，其实我何尝不羡慕你的军旅生活呢，成为军人是每个男孩子从小的梦想，当然我也不能例外。特别是看到你寄来的照片，看到部队的生活也是相当丰富多彩的，既有各种文艺活动，同时也有你发挥摄影爱好的用武之地。有些知识不一定只能在书本上才能学来，实践中得到的锻炼和提升有时更有效率。

<u>人是感情动物，总是有怀旧之情，我们今天拍摄的照片，以后都必将会成为回忆，特别是你提到的相同人物相同地点在不同时间进行拍摄的问题，我也是相当期待</u>[17]。如果真有这种照片呈现在我们面前的时候，我想应该是相当激动和感慨，两张甚至数张薄薄的照片承载了其间跨越的时间以及照片中人物的生活经历，也可能能从照片中人物的表情、动作、衣着等表象中读出天真无邪、青春活力、成熟稳重、安详平和，甚至酸甜苦辣……摄影魅力如斯，更能激励你我好好探究，多多实践，多多交流，以期共同进步吧。

边疆之地，想必此时天气已凉，也请保重，注意增加衣物。

此致，一切安好！盼复！

许　雷
1982 年 10 月 30 日于榕城

17　编者注：何博在此处划线

第 3 页

照片中的拍摄地点,五一广场的北侧门(其实就是在毛主席塑像及纪念馆的后面),我此次拍摄还要选择了于山西麓定光寺(也称白塔寺)内较有特色的定光塔(俗称白塔)为背景,并且选择了不同地点和角度两张照片,如你细看一下我上封信中寄了你的两张照片,在毛主席塑像的后面都可以看到白塔的身影。

定光塔全名报恩定光多宝塔,为福州"三山两塔"(乌山、于山、屏山和乌塔、白塔)地标之一,是闽王王审知(也就是曾给你的信中提到的闽王王延钧的父亲,为闽国的建立者)为其父母祈福,于唐天祐元年(公元904年)建造,次年才在塔南建定光寺。传说在挖塔基时,发现一颗光芒四射的宝珠,故名定光塔。明嘉靖十三年(1534年)塔被雷而毁,嘉靖二十七年(1548年)重建后,仅有原塔之半的高度,共七层,塔身用白灰粉刷,故称白塔。

第一张照片拍摄于早晨刚到定光寺之际,近几日福州也开始降温,所以晨起要穿外套了。我在寺内一也游览,一也寻找合适的拍摄地点,经过天王殿和大雄宝殿,当来到法雨堂时,发现白塔可清晰

公文纸

第45页

映入眼帘，于是选取个己的角度，取景构图，因法雨堂前空地较窄，所以只能用仰拍，这样也正好将白塔完整的收入镜头了。我此次是以照片左侧的枯树作为参照，设置好相机后我就先靠着树枝站到了右边，现在看来，效果还算满意吧。拍完这张照片后继续游览，发现寺内可游览的地方甚多，不知不觉已到午间，天气变热，遂除去外套在榕寿岩旁的石凳休息，发现在此处看去，白塔也清晰可见，且正好旁边有古榕相衬，景致甚好。于是趁休息之际不断琢磨如何取景构图，发现从我所处的位置望向白塔，正好有一石栏杆挡住白塔底部，于是想着拍照时干脆舍弃白塔底部，我坐在石栏上，只取石栏以上部分，而且水平的石栏还可以作为构图时一个很好的参照。于是拍摄时将取景器底线和石栏的上沿水平对齐，调好焦，定好时间，我坐到石栏上进行了拍摄。因使用的是后置相机，当时疏忽了视差，所以部分石栏最终还是呈现在了照片中，不过我想这种稍微有点"意外"的效果倒是让我感觉更好。试想，如果真像我预想的那样完全舍弃石栏，最终我是一个坐木桨的

"漂浮"状态，无所依靠，倒会显得怪异。我想，这也是摄影本身能给我们带来惊喜的原因吧。我们构建想象，用心拍摄，但关需要等一阵子，冲洗后拿到照片才能真正看到照片拍摄的效果，先不管效果是好是坏，只是拿到照片的那一刻，我们的内心就充盈了期待的喜悦。

你信中提到羡慕我的工作，其实我何偿不羡慕你的军旅生活呢，成为军人是每个男孩子从小的梦想，当然我也不能例外，特别是看到你寄来的照片，看到部队人的生活也是相当丰富多彩的，既有各种文艺活动，同时也有你发挥摄影爱好的用武之地，有些知识，不一定只能在书本上才能学来，实践中得到的锻炼和提升有时更有效率。

人是感情动物，总有怀旧之情，我们今天拍摄的照片，以后都终将成为回忆，特别是你提到的相同人物相同地点，在不同时间进行拍摄的问题，我也是相当期待，如果真有这种照片呈现在我们面前的时候，我想应该是相当激动和感慨，两张甚至数张薄薄的照片承载了其间跨越的时间以及照片中人物的生活经历，也可能

第 6 页

能从照片中人物的表情动作、衣着等考察出读书、天真无邪、青春活力、成熟稳重、宁静平和，甚至酸甜苦辣……。摄影魅力如斯，更能激励你我好好探究、多多实践、多多交流，以期共同进步吧。

边疆之地，想必此时天气已凉，也请保重，注意增加衣物。

此致，一切安好！盼复！

许雷
1982年10月30日于榕城

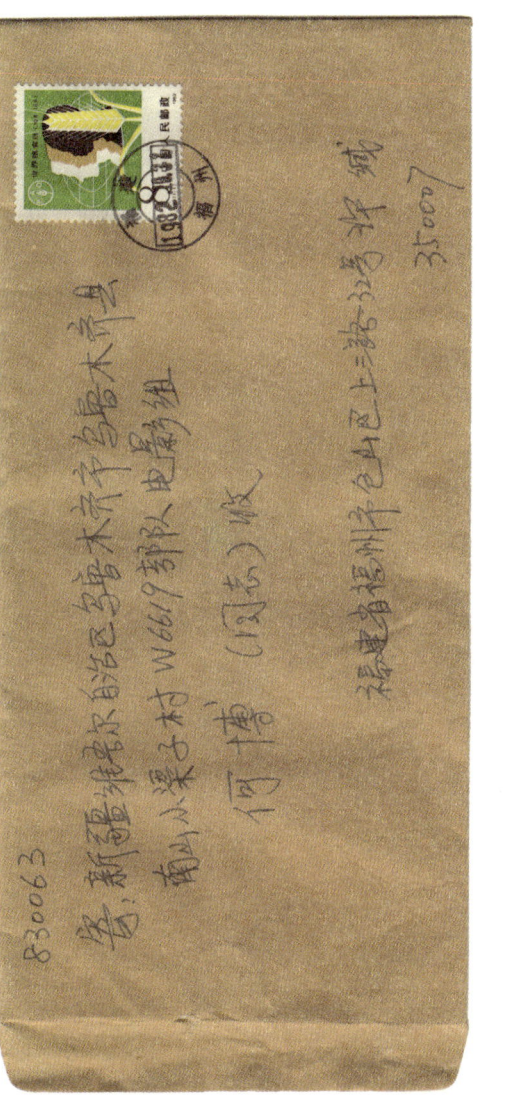

Dear He Bo,

I hope you're doing well.

Thank you for your kind words. Fujian is prone to typhoons, so we are actually pretty used to them. Since we live in the downtown area, it will be fine if we stay indoors until the typhoon passes, so don't worry.

You said in your letter that we would take on a new role as subject or performer while we enter the frame after setting up the camera. This interpretation makes a lot of sense to me.

The role of the subject is objectively inescapable in the context of photography, whereas that of the performer is our conscious decision. When we're in front of the camera, we always want to present our best selves. To put it another way, we always have an imagined self that we try to show to the camera. That's why, especially in the case of self-portrait, I feel like I'm performing.

At the moment of setting up the camera, we've already started the process of constructing this imagined self. It gradually gains clarity as we step into the frame and only vanishes when we press the shutter. This entire process is relatively long and we're directly involved, so the mental activities we must go through while taking a self-portrait are considerably more complicated than having our photo taken by others.

In your previous letter, you also mentioned how the change of space and the number of people would affect the result. Let's take the photos I'm sending you this time and before as examples. I don't think there's any fixed pattern for self-portraits.

However, after seeing so many souvenir photos, they have left some impression on me and I may intentionally or unintentionally incorporate that format in my own works. I sometimes even ask the photo lab staff to mark the location and date of shooting onto my works as what they usually do with conventional souvenir photos. Yet, if you look closely at my facial expression in those photos, instead of being impassive, they're rather more relaxed and chill since I really enjoyed the entire process and was fully immersed in it. The kind of souvenir photos for tourists, on the other hand, is usually taken in a rush under the direction of the photographer, capturing nothing but seriousness or doubt.

This time, the two photographs I'm sending you were taken a few days ago at Yu Mountain in Fuzhou, which is a massive area with many unique attractions. It's on the northern side of Wuyi Square, right behind the Chairman Mao statue and the Memorial Hall.

I chose the Dingguang Pagoda (also known as the White Pagoda) inside the Dingguang Temple (also known as the White Pagoda Temple) at the west of the mountain foot as background. I also picked different locations and angles for the two photos respectively. You may also see the White Pagoda behind Chairman Mao's statue, if you take a closer look at my last two photos.

The full name of Dingguang Pagoda is the Bao'en Dingguang Tahoto Pagoda. It is one of the five landmarks in Fuzhou, which includes Wu Mountain, Yu Mountain, Ping Mountain, the Black Pagoda, and the White Pagoda.

The pagoda was built by Wang Shenzhi, Emperor Taizu of Min, in the name of his parents during Tang Dynasty (904 AD). The following year, the Dingguang Temple was constructed to the south of the pagoda. Wang Shenzhi was the founder of the Min Kingdom and the father of Wang Yanjun who is also mentioned in my previous letter. According to legend, a radiant pearl was discovered when laying the foundation for the tower, hence the name Dingguang, meaning "anchoring light" in Chinese. The pagoda was struck by lightning and destroyed in 1534. It was only half the original size when it was reconstructed in 1548. It's also known as the White Pagoda since it was later painted with lime.

The first photo was taken when I arrived at the Dingguang Temple in the morning. The temperature has recently dropped here, so I had to put on a jacket.

As I walked around the temple, I was looking for a

suitable location for my self-portrait. After passing through the Hall of Heavenly Kings and the Main Hall of Great Might, I finally arrived at the Hall of Dharma Rain where I found the White Pagoda standing in front of me.

Then I began searching for the ideal angle and framing for my photos. Due to the limited space in front of the Hall of Dharma Rain, I finally decided to shoot at a low angle to capture the entirety of White Pagoda. I first chose the tree on the left as my reference and set up the camera accordingly. Then I entered the frame and stood on the right side of the tree. Now that I think about it, this composition turned out just fine.

I resumed my tour of the Dingguang Temple after taking this photo. But there was so much to see, I didn't realize it was already midday until I had to take off my jacket because of the heat.

To catch my breath, I rested on a stone bench next to Rongshou Rock and discovered by chance that I had a clear view of the White Pagoda from where I was. Additionally, the pagoda and the ancient banyan on the side formed a lovely image. So, as I sat on the bench, I kept thinking about how to frame the scene.

The bottom of the pagoda was blocked by a stone railing from my point of view. It was natural to sit on the railing and capture what was above it while ignoring what was below. Furthermore, the railing served as a helpful reference for composition. All I had to do was align the bottom line of the viewfinder with the stone railing's upper border.

Then I set up the camera and sat on the railing for the photo. I was, however, using a rangefinder camera and had forgotten about the parallax problem. As a result, a portion of the stone railing has entered the frame, which actually looks better than I expected. If it was completely out of the frame, it would seem as if I was floating with no support beneath me, which would be rather bizarre.

I think this is exactly why photography is always full of surprises. After all the anticipation and effort we put into our work, we still have to wait a little longer for the film to develop before seeing the final result. No matter how it turns out, we are always excited to find out what our hard work has accomplished.

You said you find my job appealing, but in fact I also find your military life fascinating. Every man dreams of being a soldier when he is a little boy, and I am no exception. Your photos have revived my passion for it, especially now that I realize how colorful military life can be, with so many cultural and artistic activities. Meanwhile, you can also put your photography skills to use, which is fantastic because certain skills can be acquired more efficiently through practice in real life than through books.

Humans have feelings, one of which is nostalgia, easily triggered by the photos we take because today's photos will eventually become tomorrow's memories. I'm also excited to photograph the same people in the same location but at different times, as you suggested. If such photos are presented to me, I can totally see myself being overcome with emotions.

It's incredible how these small photographs can convey so much, such as the passage of time between two stages in life and the various stories behind. On the surface of photos, we see their faces, gestures, and clothing, but all of them together invites us to rediscover something deeper, which could be the innocence of childhood, the boundless energy of youth, the maturity of adulthood, and all of life's ups and downs...... And this is precisely the charm of photography, and it motivates us to keep discovering, practicing, and continuing this conversation so that we can make progress together in the future.

That's it for now. I suppose it's getting cold at the borders. Take good care of yourself.

Until next time,

Xu Lei
October 30, 1982, Fuzhou

8
八

The Fourth Letter from He Bo

许雷兄：

得知台风对你在甚至影响，甚慰。此番回信，因连队信纸未及时采购，故只能一行书写，望见谅。

谈及镜头前之表演，我看说有意思的自拍行为，我认为你用"想象，一词来形容甚是贴切，通过设置各种可以控制的因素而来实现所想状态（或者说尽可能状态），另外，我在实践的过程中也比较切实地体会到你所说的这到抑下快门，这种想象了多制消退。"所以我感觉，在自拍时，自我想象永远一无法百分之百地具象化，这可以他人为对象来进行导演摄影还不一样。前摄他人，摄影者无须在两种身份（米去）之间转换，但自拍不然；最是表演，但终究无法尽性而为，要顾及许多真实的问题：如我赠你的数张照片中，始终有焦点不实之虞，确实难以在沉浸于摆拍与表演之牛的同时理智地再告派自己干的本身

来自何博的第四封信

许雷兄：

得知台风对你无甚影响，甚慰。此番回信，因连队信纸未及时采购，故只能两行挤作一行书写，望兄见谅。

谈及镜前之表演，或者说有意识的自拍行为，我认为你用"想象"一词来总结甚是贴切，通过设置各种可以控制的因素来实现所想状态（或者说尽可能实现）。另外，我在实践的过程中也比较切实地体会到你说的"直到按下快门，这种想象才急剧消退"。所以我感觉，在自拍时，自我想象永远无法百分之百地具象化，这与以他人为对象来进行导演摄影还不一样。拍摄他人，摄影者无须在两种身份（状态）之间转换，但自拍不然。虽然是"表演"，但终究无法尽性而为，要顾及许多实打实的问题：如我赠你的数张照片中，始终有焦点不实之虞，确实难以在沉浸于摆拍与表演之乐的同时理智地再告诉自己干的本身仍然是一项技术活儿。

你在信中谈到你在福州各地自拍之时，都以留念照的形态来处理，我也在你赠我的照片里发现了这个特点，而这种模式确实能在许多地方见到。人们在某处景点或具有纪念性的地点拍照时，总会以某种习惯性的仪式心态来对待，我家中老照片里有很多都是这样的。

我父辈年代，摄影器材相当难得，只因父亲是县政府宣传部门的工作人员，才有些机会为自己家人和密友拍摄一些留念照。这些照片里难见笑容，反倒是更早的照片中，父辈儿时的画面里，笑迹可循。不知缘因为何，或许是年纪越大，越没有什么可乐之处了吧。

看你给我的照片，依信中文字为线索，仿佛自己也置身现场。信中对拍摄细节的描述着实有画面感。你谈到使用旁轴相机拍摄时，因视差而产生的"意外"非常有意思。这不正是之前提到的，在控制和表演的自觉性之外的那种（那些）不受掌控的因素么？很多时候，这些意外都被当成废片扔了，但我觉得可惜，于是会把我不小心按下快门捕获的影像收集起来。这次赠你的两张照片便是我在组织与战友或友人的合影时不慎触发快门而诞生的"废片"。

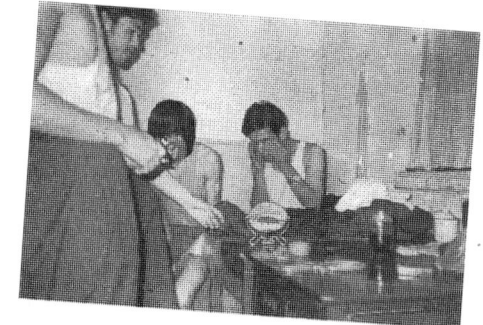

第一张是我今年夏天与战友在营房休息时拍摄的。那时无出操、训练，亦无演出任务，我便建议另三位战友一道，以最为闲适的状态合影。照片拍摄之前，我坐在椅子上，右手捏着快门线，身旁的维吾尔战友克里木正在按揉眼睛——他歌唱得好，但眼睛不好。这时，焦钢（之前照片中出现过）放了个屁，我被逗得笑了，手一抖，按下了快门线上的触发开关。焦钢（画面左边）和战友张阿毛也被捕捉了下来。

仿佛是一项我未溶凡。

你在信中谈到你在福州各地拍之时，都以幻县念照的形态来处理，我也在你赠我的照片里发现了这个特点。而这种模式的确实能在许多地方见到。人们在某处景点或具有纪念性的地点拍照时，总会因自某种习惯性的心态来对待，我家中老照片里有很多都是这样的。我父辈年轻时，遇到要拍相当难得，只因父辈是县政府官僚部门些作人员，才有些机会为自己家人和家友拍摄一些留念型照呼片里难见笑容，反倒是更早的照片中，父辈儿时的画置里，笑迹可循。不知缘因为何，或许是年纪越大越没有什么可乐之处了吧。

看你给我的照片，后信中文字为线索，仿佛自己也置身现场。信中对拍摄细节的描述着实有回画度。你说到使用旁轴相机拍摄时，因视差而产生的意外，非常有意思。这不正是之前提到的在拍到和表

　　第二张亦是夏天，不过是去年。那是我们在乌鲁木齐市里进行汇报演出的间隙，与战友及在市里学习、工作的朋友们结伴前往人民公园游玩。人民公园有一湖，众人议定泛舟湖上。我便将随身携带的相机架好，提议大家一起合影留念。我亦入镜，故将相机连上了快门线。时值公园工作人员调整船的缆绳，我们在岸边等候。由于前一天演出甚为疲乏，当日游览也是呵欠连连。等待之中，也许是神迹恍惚，触发了快门。彼时其他人都专注于小船，故无人盯视镜头，仅我在按下快门后乍醒。现在想来，这不仅是自拍，更[18]是一张抓拍，甚至偷拍了。呵呵。

　　这两张照片在我看来，没有光鲜的亮点，也没有形式层面的美或者"好看"，但却是快门开合那一瞬间，包括我自身在内的所有人毫不刻意状态的呈现。这确是一种"真实"[19]：它是在人们将要收起放松的状态进行摆拍之前的缓冲，也是从知道要拍合影开始，最没有防备的真实。庸懒、戏谑、漠然、无聊、激动……就像是不同人等着上台领奖时的各异状态。这种无心插柳之得也不常有，我也不打算只把它们视为调剂或佐料。细而想之，这些时刻中留存的影像，或许才是我们的"日常"最为具有说服力的证据或者痕迹。

　　你的信中最后提到"回忆"，着实是个大话题，我就留待下一封信里再详细说说我的看法吧。

　　末了，有一想法，不知许雷兄觉得妥否：如若今后有机会能亲自面见兄，是否可以一同自拍合影一张？想必很有意思。

　　边疆入冬，衣物被褥极厚，体感舒适，谢兄叮嘱！望兄工作顺利，另祝嫂、侄安康！

　　盼复！

何　博

1982 年 11 月 10 日于乌鲁木齐南山

18　编者注：此处删去了原文中"准确"二字
19　编者注：此处删去了原文中"真实"后，"是许多类不同真实中的一种"一句

演的自觉性之外的渐变，那些，不受掌握的因素么？很多时候，这些意外都被当成废片扔了，但我觉得可惜，于是会把我不小心按下快门捕捉的影像收集起来。这次赠你的两张照片便是我在挑识与成为友人的合影时不慎触发快门而诞生的"废片"。

第一张是我今年夏天与成友在营房休息时拍摄的。那时无山撑、训练、布演出任务，我便建议另三位成友一道，以成为词造的状态合影。照片拍摄之前，我坐在椅子上，右手握着快门线，身旁的作品字与成友无正在摆擦眼睛——他歌唱得好，但眼睛不好。催时，焦钢面面走过，和成友张阿毛也被抓拍了下来。

第二张亦是夏天，不过是去年。那天，我们在乌鲁木齐市里进行汇报演出的间隙，与成友及在市里实习亨之徐的朋友们结伴前往人民公园游玩。人民公园在一湖，众人议定泛舟湖上。我便将随身携带的相机架好，提议大家一起合影留念。我亦入镜，故将相机连上了快门线。时值公园工作人员调整船的缆绳，我们在出发等候。由于前二天演出甚为疲惫，当日游览也是呵欠连连，等待之中也许是神迟悦惺触发了快门。瞬时其他人都专注于小船，故无人盯视镜头，仅我在镜下快门后左顾。现在想来，这不仅是自拍，更准确是一抓拍，甚至偷拍了。呵呵。

这两张照片在我看来，没有光鲜的亮点，也没有那求层面的美或者雅者，但却是快门开合那一瞬间包括我自身在内的所有人毫不刻意状态的呈现。这确是一种"真实"，是许多类不同真实中的一种：记是在人们将要收起放松的状态而行抒抱之间的绞神，也是从知道要拍合影开始最没有防备的真实。慵懒、戏谑、漠然、□□激劲……无聊

就像是不同人等产上台领奖时的各异状态，这种无心插柳之得也不常有，我也不打算白白把它们视为调
心
4

刻或佐料。细而想之，日及时刻中现存的影像，或许才是我们的"日常"最为具有说服力的证据或者痕迹。你的信中最后提到"回忆"，着实是个大话题，我就留下一封信里再详细说说我的看法吧。

末了，有一想法不知许甫兄觉得如否：如若今后有机会能亲自面见兄，是否可以共同自拍合影一张？想必很有些意思。

边疆入冬，衣物被褥极厚，你感受得住，谢兄叮嘱！望兄诸顺利，另祝嫂、侄安康！

盼复！

何博

1982年11月10日于乌鲁木齐南山。

5

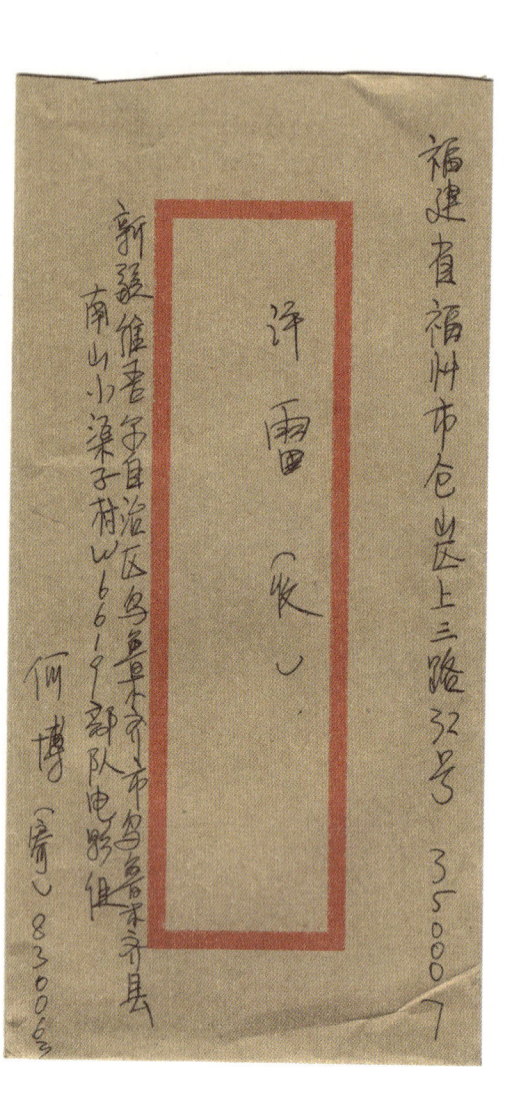

Xu Lei

He Bo

Dear Xu Lei,

I am glad to learn that the typhoon did not affect you much. Since my company did not purchase letter papers in time, I have to cram my words together to save some space in this one. Please excuse my crowded handwriting.

Speaking of performing in front of the camera, or the conscious act of taking a self-portrait, I think you've summed it up very well with the phrase "imagined self," an ideal state obtained by exerting as much control over various elements as possible.

I also have experienced in practice what you mean when you said, "It (the imagined self) only vanishes when we press the shutter." That's why, I believe that our self-imagination will never be perfectly visualized with self-portraits. Unlike directing and photographing others, the photographer is not required to switch between two identities (states of mind), as is the case when photographing oneself.

It's doomed to be a sort of performance that can't be done freely because there are always small issues that need our attention, such as out of focus in the photos I've sent you. It is indeed not an easy job to enjoy myself in the performance while also paying attention to the technical side of photography.

You said that you had been taking self-portraits in the form of souvenir photos all across Fuzhou. This form, which is fairly popular, has indeed caught my attention. People often approach taking a souvenir photo at tourist attractions or monumental landmarks as something formal, which explains the style of many of my father's old photographs.

Camera equipment was rare in his generation. My father only had the opportunity to take souvenir photos of his family and close friends because he worked in the county government's propaganda department. I also realize that smiles are quite rare to come by in his photos, though there are traces of them in some old ones from his childhood. I'm not sure why that's the case; perhaps it becomes more difficult to see the child in you as time passes by.

I feel like I am there with you as I look at the photos you sent me and follow your words as clues. Especially since your detailed descriptions of your shooting process have created for me a really vivid image. The parallax "surprise" caused when shooting with a rangefinder camera is indeed a beautiful accident. Isn't this exactly the kind of uncontrollable factor outside of the conscious performance as mentioned before?

Many times, these "accidents" are discarded, which is such a waste, therefore I decided to collect these unexpected moments taken by hitting the shutter accidentally. The two photographs I'm sending you this time are both "accidents" that were made when the shutter was released unexpectedly while arranging a group portrait with my comrades and friends.

The first one was taken this summer when I was taking a break in the barracks with my comrades. There was no drill, no training, and no performance, so I invited three of them to join me for a group portrait to show our most relaxed state. Before the photo was taken, I was sitting on a chair with the cable release in my right hand, and my Uighur comrade Krimu beside me was rubbing his eyes - he has a lovely voice, but poor eyesight. Jiao Gang (who had appeared in the prior shots)

passed gas at that very moment, and I was so amused that my hand trembled and triggered the cable release. Both Jiao Gang (on the left) and my comrade Zhang Amao were captured in the photo.

The second one was taken last summer. During the break between our performances in Urumqi, I went on a trip to People's Park with my comrades and friends who were studying

and working in the city.

In the People's Park, there was a lake where we decided to sail together. Then I set up the camera I had brought with me and proposed that we take a group photo together. I was supposed to be in it as well, so I used a cable release. We waited on the shore while park staff adjusted a boat's mooring line. I was exhausted from yesterday's performance and couldn't stop yawning throughout the trip. As we were waiting, I triggered the shutter almost in a trance. Everyone else was preoccupied with the boat, so no one except me, awakened right after the accident, was looking at the camera. Now that I think about it, it was more of a snapshot, or even a sneak shot, than a group portrait, which is amusing.

There is no special highlight in these two photographs, which, in my opinion, aren't even "good photos" at first glance. But they do catch the natural state of us in the split second between the shutter opening and shutting. Out of all the numerous sorts of realities, a specific kind of reality is thus captured: it's a buffer before getting ready for a pose, or even the most unguarded state of mind with no intention of being photographed. It's a state of being relaxed, playful, indifferent, bored, excited, etc., which is like the suspense before receiving an award on stage, and it varies depending on the person. Such unintentional gains don't come around often, and I'm not going to put them aside. The more I think about it, the more I believe that photographs shot at unexpected times provide the most persuasive evidence and remnants of our everyday life.

At the end of your letter, you talked about "memory", which is another huge topic. I prefer to leave it at that for the time being and try to expand on it in my next letter.

By the way, I have one last thing to ask: If we get the opportunity to meet in person in the future, would you like to take a self-portrait together? It will certainly be worthwhile.

It's already wintertime at the border. I'm switching to thicker clothing and bedding with ease. Thank you for reminding me of the weather change.

Sending you all my best wishes. Talk soon!

Cheers,

He Bo
November 10, 1982, Nanshan, Urumqi

9
九

The Fifth Letter from Xu Lei

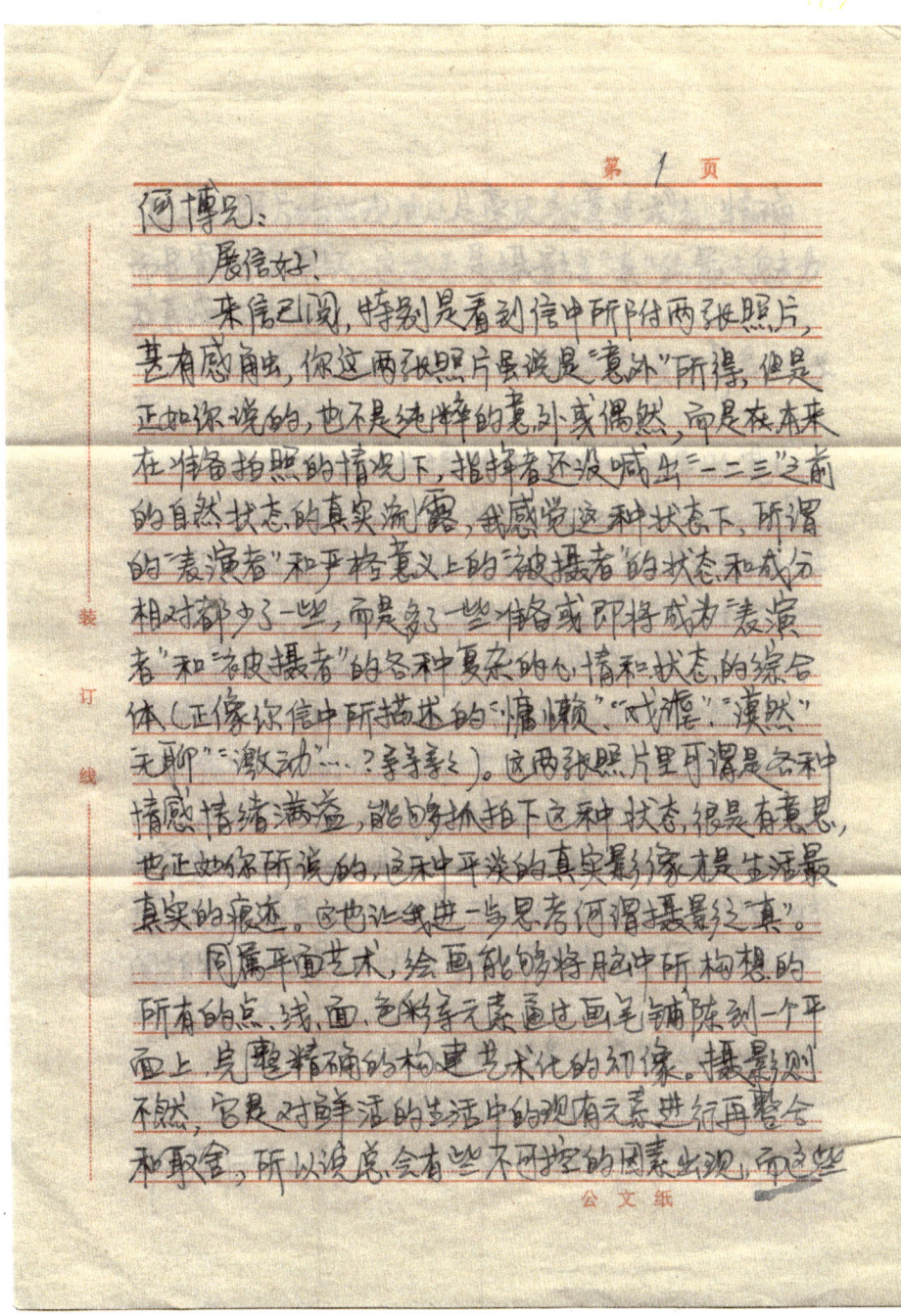

第 1 页

何博兄：

展信好！

来信已阅，特别是看到信中所附两张照片，甚有感触。你这两张照片虽说是"意外"所得，但是正如你说的，也不是纯粹的意外或偶然，而是在本来在准备拍照的情况下，指挥者还没喊出"一二三"之前的自然状态的真实流露。我感觉这种状态下，所谓的"表演者"和平常意义上的"被摄者"的状态和成分相对都少了一些，而是多一些准备或即将成为"表演者"和"被摄者"的各种复杂的心情和状态的综合体（正像你信中所描述的"慵懒"、"戒惧"、"漠然"、"无聊"、"激动"……？等等等等）。这两张照片里可谓是各种情感情绪满溢，能够抓拍下这种状态，很是有意思。也正如你所说的，这开中平淡的真实影像捕获生活最真实的痕迹。它也让我进一步思考何谓"摄影之真"。

同属平面艺术，绘画能够将脑中所构想的所有的点、线、面、色彩等元素通过画笔铺陈到一个平面上，是更精确的构建艺术化的初像。摄影则不然，它是对鲜活的生活中的现有元素进行再整合和取舍，所以说总会有些不可控的因素出现，而这些

公 文 纸

来自许雷的第五封信

何博兄：

展信好！

来信已阅，特别是看到你信中所附的两张照片，甚有感触。你这两张照片虽说是"意外"所得，但是正如你说的，也不是纯粹的意外或者偶然，而是本来在准备拍照的情况下，指挥者还没有喊出"一二三"之前的，自然状态的真实流露。我感觉这种状态下，所谓的"表演者"和严格意义上的"被摄者"的状态和成分相对都少了一些，而多了一些准备或即将成为"表演者"和"被摄者"的各种复杂的心情和状态的综合体（正像你信中所描述的"慵懒"、"戏谑"、"漠然"、"无聊"、"激动"……）。这两张照片里可谓是各种情感情绪满溢，能够抓拍下这种状态很是有意思，也正如你所说的，这种平淡的真实影像才是生活最真实的痕迹。这也让我进一步思考何谓摄影之"真"。

同属平面艺术，绘画能够将脑中所构想的所有的点、线、面、色彩等元素通过画笔铺陈到一个平面上，完整精确地构建艺术化的幻象摄影则不然，它是对鲜活的生活中的现有元素进行再整合和取舍，所以说总会有些不可控的因素，而这些"意外"照片的出现也正是毫无刻意追求去[20]精确而显露出的真实，这也正是摄影之"真"的最大的魅力和真谛所在吧。

此次寄于你的在金山寺的合影，应该也算是一张意外所得之照吧。

之前给你的信中提到过约翰·汤姆逊其人，也提到我想去探访其拍摄过的地方并自拍留影。近一段时间我一直在查阅相关资料，并且趁闲暇时间探访了部分约翰·汤姆逊当年拍摄过的地方，包括此次寄于你的照片中的拍摄地点金山寺、方广岩。

前面信中我们讨论过同一个（批）人在同地点不同时间拍照的问题，而我能探访约翰·汤姆逊在一百多年前就拍过照的地方并且也拍下照片，心情相当感慨，这算是相同地点不同的拍摄者在不同的时间拍照。摄影可以在多种维度中将不同的人和事联系在一起。

说到金山寺，很多人都以为是江苏镇江白娘子"水漫金山"之地。其实在福州闽江之中也有一座水中寺庙曰金山寺，此寺建于宋代绍兴年间（1131年），现有的建筑是民国年间重建的。寺院小巧玲珑，四面临水，环境清幽，别有天地，自古便受到旅闽人士的厚爱，当然，约翰·汤姆逊也是其中之一，

---

20 编者注：此处许雷在"追求"与"去"之间加入对调号

第 2 页

"意外"照片的出现也不是毫无刻意追求这、精确而是露出的真实，这也正是摄影之"真"的最大魅力和真谛所在吧。

此次寄于你的有金山寺的合影，应该也算是一张意外所得之照吧。

之前给你的信中提到过约翰·汤姆逊其人，也提到我想去探访约翰其拍摄过的地方并自拍留影。近一段时间我一直在查阅相关资料，并且趁闲暇时间探访了部分约翰汤姆逊当年拍摄过的地方。此次寄于你的照片中的拍摄地点金山寺、方广岩均为约翰·汤姆逊当年在福州拍摄过的地点。前面的信中我们讨论过同一个(批)人在同地点，不同时间拍照的问题。而我能去探访约翰汤姆逊在100多年前就拍过照的地方并且也拍下照片，心情也是相当感慨，这算是相同地点，不同的拍摄者在不同的时间拍照。摄影可以在多种维度中将不同的人和事联系在一起。

谈到金山寺，很多人都以为是江苏镇江的娘子"永漫金山"之地。其实在福州闽江之中也有一庙水中寺庙曰金山寺，此寺建于宋代绍兴年间(1131年)，现有

公 文 纸

可贵的是，还给我们留下了她一百多年前的艳影。

周六下午我约了几个同事一道前往金山寺游览，刚到渡口位置，同事们就被金山寺的美景所触动了，吵着要拍照。除我之外，同去的同事吴晓山也带了相机，所以我们就各自准备给大家拍照。我想架好相机，给所有人拍一张合影，而吴晓山没带三角架，只好自己拿着相机拍摄取景[21]。我一直忙于架设相机调整取景和参数，吴晓山其间已经招呼其他三名同事选好了位置并摆好造型准备拍了。

这时他们几人一直在招呼我过去同拍，于是我开启了自拍器，跑到他们中间站好。我站定后，吴晓山也没有马上拍摄，而是又端着相机仔细地调整了一番取景，就当他刚刚按下快门后，我的相机也响起了"咔嚓"声，两者几乎是同时拍摄的。

吴晓山拍摄的时候一直在招呼大家看镜头，而我的相机则是孤零零地站在那里以定时自拍模式进行拍摄。期间我惦念着我的相机何时拍摄，所以一直看着它，于是最终照片上除了我之外，其他人都是望向吴晓山的相机且均为严肃认真的拍照状态，就有了这么一张"自拍"和"他拍"的合体照片。从照片里我的表情状态和他人表情状态的对比之中，也可以看出我们之前讨论的自拍和他拍的一些区别吧。这张照片整体上对于我来说可能是一张自拍的"意外"之照。而吴晓山，他本想精心导演和设计一张"正常"的留影照，但是因为我这个不可控因素的出现，让他得到了一张稍有"意外"的"正常"照。

方广岩这张照片是以方广寺为背景，拍摄于登山前往方广寺的路途中。

10月3日写给你的信中介绍过约翰·汤姆逊曾在福州鼓山涌泉寺、YUAN-FU寺等地拍摄，我对当时的资料中其他地名和景色较为熟悉，唯有此YUAN-FU寺不甚熟悉，不知在何处。

在近一段的资料查阅中，一直留意约翰·汤姆逊在YUAN-FU寺拍的几张照片，百思不得其解。前一段适逢单位组织秋游活动，前往永泰方广岩景区（永泰县为福州市下属县之一），待进入景区，看到方广寺的时候，脑中突然映出了YUAN[22]-FU寺的照片，印象中和此地甚为相像，兴奋不已。奈何未带资料，无法比对，就赶紧拍了几张照片待回去后详加对比。

登山到一半台阶之时，发现山腰有一小处平地，可以容下三角架，于是安顿好相机取好景，我就站到了镜头前。因在山上，路险地滑、难以静止站立，便顺手抱住了旁边的一棵树。快门开启，拍下了我和方广寺的留影。

从方广岩回来之后，将洗出来的方广寺的照片与资料图片进行了对比，基本一致。而且又查阅了一些相关的文史资料，资料表明：永泰县从宋元符五年（1102年）至民国三年（1914年）间名为永福县。[23] 因为谐音或者音译，也有可能是闽地之人口音或者方言问题造成的误读等，约翰·汤姆逊所拍摄及标记的YUAN-FU[23]寺应为当时所称永福的寺庙，也就是方广寺了。

照片中可见，方广寺悬空半山，极有特色。今天我们登山访寺尚觉困难，可以想象一百多年前的条件下登山拍摄应更为艰辛。抚今思古，更觉约翰·汤姆逊影像资料的珍贵和精神可嘉。

你信中提到如有机会见面并自拍合影，我也一直有此意。我想如你有休假，可来福州一游，感受一下东南闽越之地风情，也可对我寄于你的照片中的地方探访一番。当然，如有机会，我也想去体验一下边疆风情。不管在何处，我对我们的相见及共同探讨实践自拍都是相当期待的。让我们共同期盼这一天早日到来吧！

此致，顺祝一切安好！

许 雷
1982年11月25日于榕城

---

21 编者注：此处许雷在"拍摄"与"取景"之间加入对调号
22 编者注：此处"YUAN"中字母"N"为何博添加
23 何博注：此处终得解！

第 3 页

的建筑是民国年间重建的，那灵小巧玲珑，四面临水，环境清幽，别有天地，自古便受到很国人士的厚爱，当然，约翰汤姆逊也是其中之一，可贵的是，还给我们留下了她100多年前的丰姿倩影。

周六下午我约了几个同事一道前往金山寺游览，刚到渡口位置，同事们就被金山寺的美景所触动，吵着要拍照。除我之外，同行的同事吴晓山也带了相机，所以我们就各自准备给大家拍照。我想，架好相机，给所有人拍一张合影，吴晓山没带三角架，只好自己拿着相机拍摄取景。我一直忙于架设相机，调整取景和参数，而吴晓山其间已经招呼其他三名同事选好了位置并摆好造型准备拍了，这时他们几人一直在招呼我过去同拍，于是我开启了自拍器，跑到他们中间站好。我站定后，吴晓山也没有马上拍摄，而是又端着机相仔细地调整了一番取景，就在他刚刚按下快门后，我的相机也响起了"咔嚓"声，几乎是同时拍摄的。因为吴晓山拍摄的时候一直在招呼大家看镜头，而我的相机则是孤零零的站在那里以定时自拍模式进行的拍摄，期间我也一直惦念我的相机何时拍摄，所以一直以我的

第 4 页

相机为主，一直看着它，所以最终照片上除了我之外，其他人都是望向吴晓山的相机，而且表情状态，均为平常认真的拍照状态。所以就有了这么一张"自拍"和"他拍"的合体照片。从照片中我的表情状态和他人的表情状态的对比之中，也可以看出我们之前讨论的自拍和他拍的一些区别吧。这张照片整体上对于我来说可能是一张自拍的"意外"之照。而对于吴晓山来说，他本想精心导演和设计一张"正常"的合影照，但是我这个不可控因素的出现，也让他得到了一张稍有"意外"的"正常"照。

方广岩这张照片是以方广寺为背景，拍摄于登山前往方广寺的路途中。

10月3日写给你的信中介绍过约翰·汤姆逊曾在福州鼓山涌泉寺、YUAN-FU寺等地拍摄，因对当时的资料中其他地名较为熟悉，就是，唯有比YUAN-FU寺不甚熟悉，不知在何处。在近一段的资料查阅中，一直惦着约翰·汤姆逊在YUAN-FU寺拍的几张照片，百思不得其解。前一段适逢单位组织秋游活动，前往永泰方广岩景区（永泰县为福州市下属县之一），待进入景区，看到方广寺的时候，脑中突然映出了

YUA-FU寺的照片，印象中和此地甚为相像，兴奋不已，奈何却未带资料，无法比对，就赶紧拍了几张照片待回去后详加对比。待登山到一半台阶之时，发现山腰有一小处平地，可以容下三角架，于是安顿好相机取好景，我就站到了镜头前。因在山上，路险地滑又难以静止站立，于是顺手就抱住了旁边的一棵树干，快门开启，拍下了我和方广寺的合影。从方广岩回来之后，将找出来的方广寺的照片与资料图片进行双对比，基本一致，而且又查阅了一些相关的文史资料，资料表明：永泰县从宋元符五年(1102年)至民国3年(1914年)间名为永福县，因为谐音或者音译，也有可能是闽地之人口音或者方言问题造成的误读等原因，约翰汤姆逊所拍摄及标记的YUAN-FU寺应为当时所称永福的寺庙，也就是方广寺了。照片中可见，方广寺悬空半山，极有特色。今天我们登山访寺尚觉困难，可以想象100多年前的条件下登山拍摄应更为艰辛，抚今思古，更觉约翰汤姆逊影像资料的珍贵和精神可嘉。

你信中提到如有机会见面并合拍合影，我也一直有此意。我想，如你有休假，可来福州一游，感受一下东南闽越之地风情，也可对我寄于你的

（左侧批注：处终得解！）

第 6 页

照片中的地方探访一番。当然，如有机会，我也想去体验一下边疆风情。不管在何处，我对我们的相见及共同探讨实践自拍都是相当期待的。让我俩共同期盼这一天早日到来吧！

　　此致，顺祝一切安好！

许雷
1982年11月25日于榕城

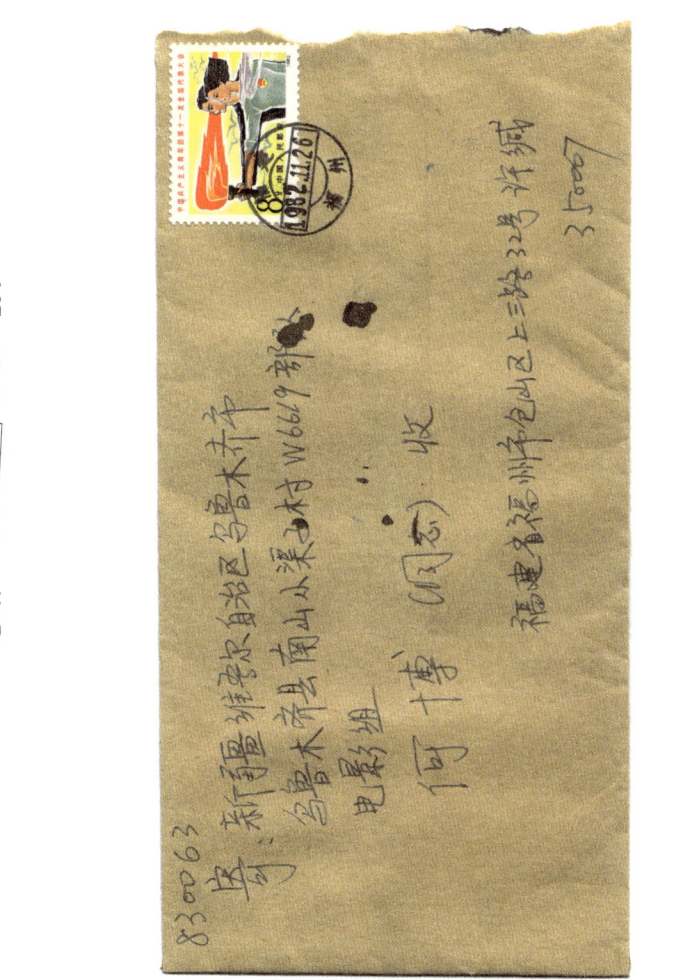

Dear He Bo,

I hope you are well and thank you for your writing.

Your two photos attached are really intriguing. They were acquired by "accident," although not entirely so, as you said. People's natural expressions were brilliantly captured before the photographer instructed them to get ready for a photo. In this case, I'd say the role of "performer" and that of "subject" in the strict sense are comparatively downplayed. Instead, in the midst of preparing to be a "performer" and a "subject," there is a flux of emotions and mental states (just as you described with words like "relaxed," "playful," "indifferent," "bored," "excited," etc.). It's a real surprise that these two photos are so emotionally charged. As you mentioned, these kinds of authentic photos in the plainness are the most loyal record of life, making me wonder what it means when we talk about the "reality" in photography.

As another type of two-dimensional art, painting is a place where all the points, lines, colors, and other elements envisaged in the mind are recreated on the base with a brush, forming an artistic imagination with integrity and precision. Photography, on the other hand, integrates or selects existing elements in real life, providing room for uncontrollable factors.

These photos taken by "accident" were not made with a deliberate pursuit of precision in the first place, and as a result, they end up disclosing a certain kind of authenticity, which is probably the greatest charm and the true meaning of "reality" that photography provides.

This time, the photo I'm sending you was also taken by "accident" at Jinshan Temple.

I think I've mentioned John Thomson in my previous letters as well as my wish to visit and take self-portraits in the places that he photographed before. Therefore, I've been doing some research and have already visited some of the places where he's been. The photographs I'm sending you are of Jinshan Temple and Fangguang Rock, both of which were captured by John Thomson in Fuzhou.

We've talked about photographing the same group of people in the same location but at different times, reminding me of what I'm doing now. Because I'm visiting and photographing the same locations that John Thomson visited and photographed over a century ago. These parallel actions make me quite emotional. Photography truly has the power to bring people and events together in multiple dimensions.

Speaking of Jinshan Temple, many people may associate it with the story of Lady White Snake from Zhenjiang in Jiangsu Province. However, the place I've been to is actually another Jinshan Temple, located in the center of the Min River in Fuzhou. This Jinshan Temple was constructed during the Song Dynasty's Shaoxing Period (1131 AD), and all of the current structures were renovated during the Republic of China. The temple is small yet exquisite, surrounded on all sides by water and offering a serene atmosphere that makes you feel like entering another world. It has always been loved by people who visit Fujian and John Thomson, of course, is also one of them. The photos that he took of the temple are so precious since they show us what it was like more than a hundred years ago.

On a Saturday afternoon, my colleagues and I visited the Jinshan Temple. They were already captivated by the view when we arrived at the ferry and wanted to have their photos taken. My colleague Wu Xiaoshan also had a camera, so we were both responsible for photographing the rest of the group. Since Wu didn't bring his tripod with him, while I was setting up mine for the group shot, he had already discovered the ideal spot and gathered three other colleagues to pose for the photo.

They invited me to join them, so I set my camera's timer and dashed over to them. When I was ready, Wu did not take the photo right away but took a while to figure out the final framing. Then, almost simultaneously with his pressing the shutter, my camera was triggered as well.

Wu directed everyone's attention to his camera, while I was thinking and looking at my own camera, standing alone on the side with the timer on. So, in the end, I was the only one looking at the camera in my photo, while everyone else was looking at Wu's camera, and they all seemed quite serious. So there you have it: a cross between a self-portrait and a portrait taken by others.

By comparing my facial expression to that of my colleagues, we may also detect some distinctions between self-portraits and portraits taken by others as we've discussed before. For me, this should also be considered an unintentional self-portrait. Wu, on the other hand, had directed the whole scene and wanted to take a "normal" group portrait, but I, the uncontrollable factor, had probably "surprised" him.

On the way to Fangguang Temple, the second photo of Fangguang Rock was taken with the temple in the background.

John Thomson had photographed Gu Mountain, Yongquan Temple, and YUAN-FU Temple in Fuzhou, as I mentioned in my letter dated October 3. All the places featured in the archives were familiar to me at the time, with the exception of YUAN-FU Temple, which I had no idea where it was.

During my recent research, I was drawn to a couple of photographs shot at the YUAN-FU temple, which perplexed me. Until a while ago, my university organized an autumn excursion to Yongtai Fangguang Rock Scenic Area (Yongtai County is one of the subordinate counties of Fuzhou City). When I entered the scenic spot and saw the Fangguang Temple, those photos of YUAN-FU Temple suddenly came to my mind. I was thrilled because they were so much like what I was seeing. Unfortunately, I didn't have them with me to compare straight away, so I quickly took some shots to compare later.

I found a platform halfway up the mountain where I could put up my tripod, so I prepared my camera and stood in front of it. It was difficult to stay still on the slippery trail. As a result, I hugged a nearby tree right before the timer was up and thus a self-portrait of myself and Fangguang Temple was captured.

I compared my photo of Fangguang Temple with those I found during my research after the trip, and they were nearly identical. I have also consulted some relevant literary and historical sources indicating that: From the fifth year of the Song Dynasty's Yuanfu period (1102) to the third year of the Republic of China (1914), Yongtai County was known as Yongfu County. John Thomson has marked the name of the temple he photographed as YUAN-FU instead of Yongfu, maybe due to some subtle twists in homonym or transliteration caused by the local accent or dialect. And Yongfu Temple is exactly today's Fangguang Temple, which is hanging halfway up the mountain in a peculiar style, as seen in the photo.

Climbing the mountain to visit the temple is still challenging today. It should have been considerably more difficult for John Thomson to do so, or even take photographs, over a century ago. When I think back on the past from today's perspective, the photos and spirit of John Thomson seem even more valuable.

Your suggestion to take a self-portrait together is exactly what I'm thinking. When you're on leave, you're welcome to visit the Min-Yue region in southeast China and check out the places featured in the photos I sent you, as well as getting a taste of the local culture yourself. And of course, I would also like to visit the border if I have the chance. No matter where we will be, I'm really looking forward to seeing you in person and exploring different kinds of self-portrait together. Let's hope that day will come soon!

Stay well,

Xu Lei
November 25, 1982, Fuzhou

The fifth letter from He Bo

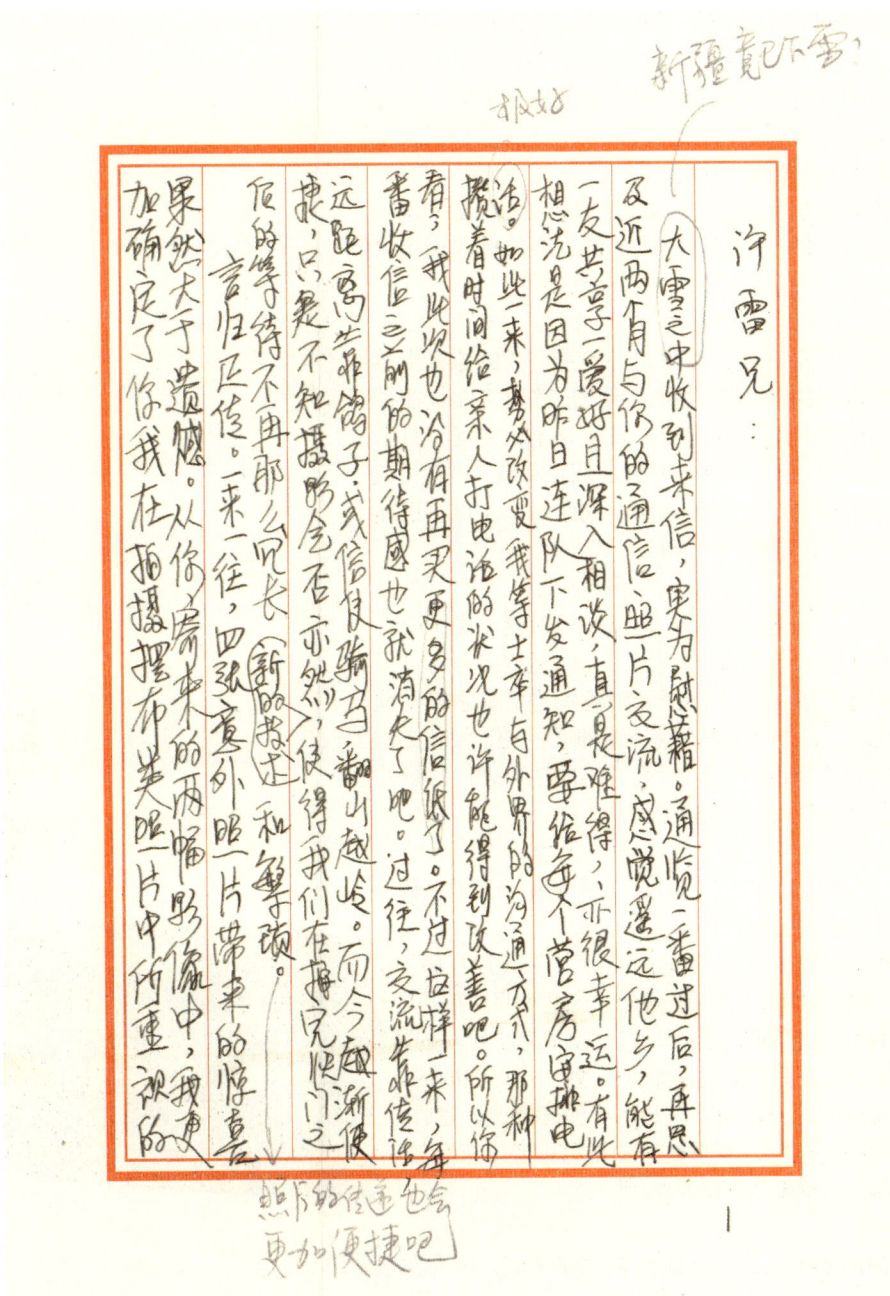

许雷兄：

大雪之中收到来信，实为慰藉。通览一番过后，再思及近两个月与你的通信、照片交流，感觉远他乡，能有一友共苦一爱好且深入相谈，真是难得，亦很幸运。有此想法是因为昨日连队下发通知，要给每个营房安排电话，如此一来，势必改变我等士卒与外界的沟通方式，那种攥着时间给亲人打电话的状况也许能得到改善吧。所以你我此次也许没有再更多的信件了。不过也这样一来，我书收信之间的期待感也就消失了吧。过往，交流是靠信件，远距离靠鸽子，或信鸽翻山越岭。而今一趟浙便捷，只是不知摄影会否亦然，使得我们在摄影兄1门之信的等待不再那么长（新的我述）和笔头言语正传。一来一往，四张意外照一片带来的惊喜。从你寄来的两幅照片像中，我更果然大于遗憾。加确定了你我在拍摄摆布类照片中所重视的

新疆竟下雪？

报好

照片的传递也会更加便捷吧

来自何博的第五封信

许雷兄：

大雪之中[24]收到来信，实为慰藉。通览一番过后，再思考近两个月与你的通信、照片交流，感觉遥远他乡，能有一友共享爱好且深入相谈，真是难得，亦很幸运。

有此想法是因为昨日连队下发通知，要给每个营房安排电话[25]。如此一来，势必改变我等士卒与外界的沟通方式，那种攒着时间给亲人打电话的状况也许能得到改善吧。所以你看，我此次也没有再买更多的信纸了。不过这样一来，每番收信之前的期待感也就消失了吧。

过往，交流靠传话，远距离靠鸽子或信使骑马翻山越岭，而今越渐便捷。只是不知摄影会否亦然，新的技术会使我们在按完快门之后的等待不再那么冗长和繁琐[26]吗？

言归正传。一来一往，四张意外照片带来的惊喜果然大于遗憾。从你寄来的两幅影像中，我更加确定了你我在拍摄摆布类照片中所重视的心理感受：从容为上，并且不只是被标准和规则所束缚。已妥善保存好你的两张写满"刻意失误"的相片，今后若再有此等无心插柳而成的影像，也不再随手丢弃，而是与所谓正常照片等而视之了。

此番读信，另一感受在于：似读一篇解谜小说，或者说一篇科普文章（后者也许更为恰当）。你通过自身考证，竟然将之前信中提到的那位英国摄影师汤姆逊所摄之未知地名的照片考证成功[27]，弟甚为佩服。尤感难得的是，你还尝试了之前我们在信中说到的在不同时间、相同地点进行拍摄的想法，以己之作呼应前人，有趣至极！

近日遇到一些事，牵涉三个人，过于纠缠，又难以解决。何事？从我给你的两张照片可知。

我跟焦钢同时喜欢上了同一个姑娘[28]，就是照片中与我趴着合影的辫子姑娘，叫做张菊芳。这两张照片都是今年早些时候拍的，与焦钢的合影是在北京故宫游玩时的留念，而跟菊芳的合影是在南山山脚的一处小景点完成的。本次未拍摄新照片，一是由于乌鲁木齐快速降温，室外较难进行相对顺畅的控制，更重要的便是因钟意菊芳而与焦钢产生的隔阂，让我无心再摸相机[29]。

菊芳是河南安阳人，与我跟焦钢同年入伍，现在在连队

24　许雷注：新疆竟已下雪？
25　许雷注：极好
26　许雷注：照片的传递也会更加便捷吧
27　许雷注：此也为乐趣所在
28　许雷注：事情变得复杂了……
29　许雷：确实烦心

以他为乐趣所在

心理感受。从容为上,并且不以是以标准的规则所来衡。已是善保存你的两张照片满,刻意以后的相片?
今后若再有此等无心插柳而成的影像,也不再随手丢弃,而是与所谓正常照片等同视之了。
此番读信,另一感发在于:似该一篇解谜小说,我自感又道又章一后者也许更为恰当。
你通过目自身来远,竟将之间信中提到的那位英国摄影师汤姆,迎所摄之来知他名的照片考察一番成功,弟甚为佩服。尤感难得的是,你还在同时间相同他乡而完了之间,我们在信中说到的在有国事!
行拮据的想法,以自己之作件与同人,有趣主板!
近日遇到一些事,本涉三人,过于纠缠,又难以解决,何事?从我给你的两张照片可知。
我跟焦钢同时喜欢上了同一个姑娘,就是照片中台我趴着合影的辫子姑娘,叫做菊芳。这两张照片都是今年早些时侯拍的,与焦钢的合影是在找寻

事情变得复杂了……

2

里负责新闻稿件的采写编辑工作，去年因报道我们电影组而与我相识，后经我介绍又与焦钢结识。之前给你去的几封信中都未曾提到此人，主要因为一切都还处于"潜伏"阶段。而就在上一封给你的信寄出后，焦钢突然告诉我，他已向菊芳表达出追求她的心意。此举让我有些手足无措，因半年前我已告诉焦钢我想要跟菊芳好的意愿，只是那时我并未看出焦钢也有同样的想法[30]。故而感觉异常无奈。

你看，照片中焦钢、菊芳，还有我的表情和状态多么舒服（至少我是这么感觉的），如今却是这般无可进退的田地。咱们总说照片上定格的细节能够确认过去那一刻的瞬间记忆，此话不假。但这次的事情更让我体会到这枚硬币的反面：当你在相反或者经历变迁之后的心境下再去看原来的照片时，这种记忆会生成相对负面的心态或者说观看效果。我越是确认在照片拍摄的那段日子里自己与另两位被摄者曾真挚地分享过快乐，就越是在"当下"感觉度日如年[31]。

算了，此事暂且不提。之前说到你我二人的自拍合影，也许很快就能实现了。连队接上级指示，今年十二月底会派一些文艺兵去往福州军区和南京军区两地进行汇报演出，近日正在征集人员中。我已向连队提出申请去往福州，若能成，定及时相告。如果你那已安有电话，请在复信中告知号码，便于联络[32]。

期待相聚！望安好！

何　博

1982年12月5日于乌鲁木齐南山

30　许雷注：藏得很深
31　许雷注：影像对记忆留存的两面性
32　许雷注：0591-8342xxxx

〔藏得很深〕

故宫游玩时的留念，而跟焦钢的照片便只是在南山山脚的一处小景点完成的。车次未拍摄新照片，一是由于乌鲁木齐快速降温，室外极难进行相对顺畅的拍摄，更重要的便是因钟萝菊芳而已焦钢产生的隔阂，让我无心再摸相机。钟实想菊芳是河南安阳人，与我很焦钢同年入伍，现在连队里负责新闻稿件的采写。钟萝菊芳去年因报道我们电影组而与我相识。后经我介绍与焦钢结识。之前给你去的九封信中都未曾提到此人，主要因为一切都还处于"潜伏"所致。而就在上一封给你的信寄出后，焦钢突然告诉我，他已经向菊芳表达出想要追求菊芳的心思。此举让我有些手足无措，因半年前我已告诉焦钢我想要跟菊芳好的意愿，只是即时我并未看出焦钢女有同样的想法。故西感觉已非常无奈。你看，照片中焦钢的菊芳，还有我的表情你就知道多么舒服（至少我是这么

3

感觉的，如今却是一般，天则进退的田地。咱们总说"片上定格的瞬间能让过去那一刻的瞬间记忆，此近不假，但这次的事情更让我体会到启发破事成反面：当你在相友或者面经历变迁之后的心境下再去看原来的照片时，定种记忆生成相对负重的心态或者说观看效果：我感悟是确认在旧片拍摄那段的日子里自己与另一位被摄者曾真挚地为之度快乐，就越是在当下，感觉度日如年。

你若么，故事暂且不提。之前说到的你我二人的自拍合影，也许很快就能实现了。连队接上级指示，八二年十一月底金派一些文艺骨干到福州军区京宁两地进行汇报演出，近日正在征集人员中。我已向连队提出申请去往福州，若能成，定又时相告。如果你那已安有电话，请在复信中告知之码，便于联络。

期待相象！往安好！

何博 1982年12月5日于鳌桥南山

054-834265.ou

影像对记忆储存的两面性

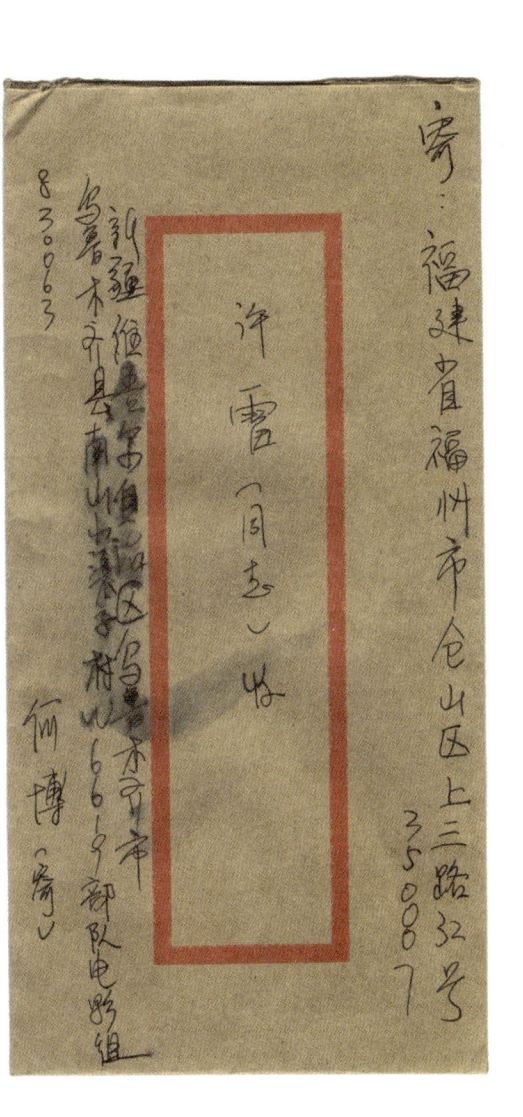

Dear Xu Lei,

Your letter genuinely warms my heart during the snow season. After reading it and reflecting on our letters and photos over the past two months, I realize how fortunate I am to have a friend like you who is equally interested in photography and willing to engage in meaningful conversations about it, despite our geographical distance.

The company just told us yesterday that each barracks will be equipped with phones. Our ways of communicating with the outside world will soon alter substantially, and we will probably no longer need to walk miles for calling our family. And that's why I also stopped buying letter papers. However, the anticipation of receiving letters will unfortunately disappear with the presence of phones.

In the old days, short-distance communication used to be done by word of mouth or messaging, while long-distance communication required pigeons or messengers riding through mountains and hills. Everything nowadays is becoming more convenient, and I'm wondering if this is the same with photography. I wish one day modern technology could save us from the long and tedious wait after pressing the shutter.

Back to business. Instead of being disappointed, the four photos in your letter and mine together amazed me. I'm more confident, based on your two photos, that we both appreciate the same psychological state depicted in staged photos and that is being at ease while not being confined by rules. I've carefully kept your two photos with "intentional mistakes." If I take any more unintended photos like these in the future, I won't discard them like before, but rather treat them like the other "regular" photos.

This time, reading your letter feels like solving a puzzle or reading a popular science article (the latter is perhaps more appropriate). I'm quite impressed that you were able to confirm the unknown location captured by the British photographer Thomson through independent research. And you also managed to put into practice our earlier idea about photographing the same location at different times, echoing the work of another photographer with your own!

I've been struggling with something that happened lately. It involves three people, which makes the situation quite complicated. You might be curious as to what it is.

The two photos I'm sending you are all about it. In short, Jiao Gang and I both fell in love with the same girl. Her name is Zhang Jufang. She is the girl with braids in the photo where she and I are both lying on the ground.

Both photographs were taken this year. The one with Jiao Gang is a souvenir photo from a trip to the Forbidden City in Beijing, and the one with Jufang was taken at a small tourist attraction at the foot of Nanshan. I didn't take any new photos this time because the temperature is dropping rapidly in

Urumqi, making it hard to control the shooting environment outside. But, more importantly, because of our shared feelings for Jufang, it's still awkward between Jiaogang and me. Therefore, I was not in the mood for taking any photos.

Jufang, who comes from Anyang in Henan Province, is in charge of writing and editing news articles in the company. The three of us were enlisted in the army in the same year. But we didn't know each other until last year when she was covering the film crew, and I introduced her to Jiao Gang later on.

I haven't mentioned her in any of my earlier letters because the situation was still fluid. After I sent you my previous letter, Jiao Gang suddenly told me that he had revealed his feelings to Jufang. I was at a loss since I told Jiao Gang just six months ago that I wanted to be with Jufang, and I had no idea that Jiao Gang had the same thought. That is why I am so frustrated now.

Look how relaxed we were in the photo (at least, that's how I felt), yet we're now in an impossible situation. It's true that the details encapsulated in a photo can help us confirm our memories of a concrete moment in the past. But this time, what happened has brought me to see the other side of the coin: Since you can get stuck in negative emotions triggered by memories if you look at old photographs when things have changed against your will. The more I treasure the good times we shared of taking those photos, the more tortured I am in the present.

But let's put that aside for now. It's possible that our wish of taking a self-portrait together will soon come true. At the end of December, the company plans to send over some crews to Fuzhou Military Region and Nanjing Military Region for special performances, and they are now looking for people to participate. I've already signed up for Fuzhou and will let you know if it works out.

I can't express how excited I am that we'll finally meet in person. If you already have a phone installed on your side, please let me know your number next time so I can call you in the future.

All the best,

He Bo
December 5, 1982, Nanshan, Urumqi

The Last Group Photo of Xu Lei and He Bo
最终的合影

About the Author

He Bo was born in the winter of 1959 in Zhongjiang County, Mianyang District, Sichuan Province. He enlisted in the army in 1980, and since then he has served in a creative team in Urumqi, Xinjiang. He enjoys singing, dancing, hosting, and photography.

Xu Lei was born in the spring of 1953 in Gaotang County, Liaocheng District, Shandong Province. He has been teaching at Fujian Normal University since 1978. He enjoys traveling and photography.

❖❖❖❖❖❖❖❖❖❖❖❖❖❖❖❖❖❖❖❖❖❖❖❖❖❖❖❖❖❖❖❖

作者小传

何博，1959年冬天出生于四川省绵阳地区中江县。1980年入伍，前往新疆乌鲁木齐某部队担任文艺兵至今。喜爱唱歌、跳舞、主持、摄影。

许雷，1953年春天出生于山东省聊城地区高唐县。1978年起任职于福建师范大学至今。爱好旅游、摄影。

Selfiers: Sealed with Images | 自拍者：尺 笺 传 影
Photographs and text © 2016   He Bo, Xu Lei | 何　博、许　雷

No part of this book may be reproduced in any manner in any media, or transmitted by any means whatsoever, electronic or mechanical (including photocopy, film or video recording, Internet posting, or any other information storage and retrieval system), without the prior written permission of the publisher.

Published by La Maison De Z
www.lamaisondez.com
info@lamaisondez.com

Art Direction: Zhen SHI
Design: 1 and 1/2 atelier Lu Min
Translation: Tang Yaxuan

First Edition of 700 copies: July 2023

ISBN: 978-2-9585094-1-5